The Five Streams

A Prophetic Message on the Unity of the Church in the End Times

Keith Intrater

© Copyright 1995 — Keith Intrater

All rights reserved. This book is protected under the copyright laws of the United States of America. This book may not be copied or reprinted for commercial gain or profit. The use of short quotations or occasional page copying for personal or group study is permitted and encouraged. Permission will be granted upon request. Unless otherwise identified, Scripture quotations are from the New King James Version of the Bible © 1982 by Thomas Nelson, Inc., Nashville, Tennessee. Used by permission. Other Scriptures are from the King James Version (KJV).

Treasure House
An Imprint of
Destiny Image
P.O. Box 310
Shippensburg, PA 17257-0310

"For where your treasure is
there will your heart be also." Matthew 6:21

ISBN 1-56043-140-7

For Worldwide Distribution
Printed in the U.S.A.

Destiny Image books are available through these fine distributors outside the United States:

Christian Growth, Inc.
Jalan Kilang-Timor, Singapore 0315

Lifestream
Nottingham, England

Rhema Ministries Trading
Randburg, South Africa

Salvation Book Centre
Petaling, Jaya, Malaysia

Successful Christian Living
Capetown, Rep. of South Africa

Vision Resources
Ponsonby, Auckland, New Zealand

WA Buchanan Company
Geebung, Queensland, Australia

Word Alive
Niverville, Manitoba, Canada

Inside the U.S., call toll free to order:
1-800-722-6774

Contents

Chapter 1	The End-Time Church	1
Chapter 2	Unity Brings Revival	23
Chapter 3	God's Answer to Alienation	43
Chapter 4	The Five Streams	61
Chapter 5	Simply Jesus	89
Chapter 6	Jewish Roots	109
Chapter 7	Oneness With God	129
Appendix	Other Streams?	145

Preface

Keith Intrater's book on the five streams is an important reflection of the heart of those of us at Tikkun Ministries. We desire the unity of the true Church. This is a passion with our leadership team. However, we believe that we cannot attain this unity unless different streams in the Body of the Messiah begin to dialogue and to understand each other. A stance of opposition does not enable us to grow beyond our sectarian limitations. Furthermore, the Church that God wants to bring forth needs the truth and not the errors that are found in all the streams. This kind of correction and blending will take place only as we lay down our swords and seek to truly hear the other with empathy. If in our insecurity we are stuck on making a position absolute, we will not grow in wisdom and maturity.

I trust that Keith's book is helpful to you in this growth. We at Tikkun Ministries have dialogued much on these streams, for these streams in various ways have influenced us. We have needed to dialogue to bring forth a greater appreciation for one another since we have been influenced differently. Thus again and again we have looked to the Bible for self-evaluation.

Daniel Juster

Chapter 1

The End-Time Church

What is God saying to us as His people in these endtimes? What is the Spirit saying to the Church?

Before we can answer these questions, we must first determine what the Church is. By "the Church" I refer to the remnant of people in every nation and ethnic group who are born again and who have submitted themselves to the Lordship of Jesus. I am *not* referring to any particularly identifiable organization or structure.

In Israel today, for example, are large cathedrals of ancient churches. Most Israelis, when they hear of the words *Christian Church*, think of these medieval-style cathedrals and institutions. Also, given the history of the Crusades, the Inquisition, the Holocaust, and so on, it was difficult for me, as a Jew, to gain a positive view of the Church.

Discerning the True Church

What history books call the Christian Church often was not the Church at all. Likewise a newspaper report today of what is happening in religious circles would probably miss entirely what is going on with the true Body of Believers.

Both historical analysis and modern journalism are oblivious to what the true Church is and who the people are who compose it. Thus it is difficult to find a truthful and accurate portrayal of the body of believers throughout the past 2,000 years. It is difficult even to find out through the media what is happening with believers and revival movements in other countries today. The secular press does not give much coverage to the explosive church-growth movement in Korea, to the mass evangelism campaigns in Africa, to the hunger of the Soviet peoples for Bibles, or to the pentecostal revivals going on in Latin America.

Of course, we do not refer to a church building with "the Church," either. We do not go to the church for a worship service; we *are* the Church. We gather together in a building for worship.

Neither do I refer, by "the Church," to a local assembly under a given pastor and elders. I choose to refer to that subsection of the Church as a *congregation* in order to differentiate it from the international body of believers.

> *For when one says, "I am of Paul," and another, "I am of Apollos," are you not carnal?*
> 1 Corinthians 3:4

Here Paul wrote to the Corinthian believers that it was a carnal attitude on their part to associate themselves so exclusively with one particular leader that, in their eyes, the other sections of the Church were invalid.

We Are One Body

By definition, the Church is a body. The Church is essentially one. The mere fact that we are a body of people lumps us into one group. Spiritually speaking, sectarianism is impossible. (The Bible does indicate, however, that when falsehoods exist within the Church, there must be temporary divisions so the truths and falsehoods can be separated [see 1 Cor. 11:18-19].)

In God's eyes, we, His people, are one. It is not so much that we endeavor to become one, as it is we need to accept and respond appropriately to the fact that we already are. A husband and wife are one. They may not act as if they are one—they may fight and make life miserable for one another—but they are bound together in oneness whether they like it or not. So it is with the Church.

God desires to speak a message to us as a Church as a whole. He would like to address as one the corporate body of people who are called by His name. Unfortunately, due to our divisiveness, it has largely been impossible for God to address us as one body. People have listened to God as individuals; at times a local congregation has been able to discern His will; and on rare occasions even a whole denomination has heard His voice.

The Five Streams

However, the international Body of Christ has not been able to respond as one unit.

The Effect of Media and Communications

Due to the times we live in, it is inevitable that a new unity will arise in the Body of Christ. Already there is an ever-increasing one-world unity movement in the economic and political realm.

But you, Daniel, shut up the words, and seal the book until the time of the end; many shall run to and fro, and knowledge shall increase.

Daniel 12:4

The Bible clearly predicted that in modern times communication and transportation systems would rapidly increase. Mega-trend analysts refer to the time we live in today as the "Information Age."

Any place on the globe is quickly becoming a mere flick-of-the-switch away. Products are marketed internationally as easily as they are at the next town down the road. People are beginning to identify themselves internationally with movements and ideologies more than they are with their own ethnic group.

These trends have affected the Body of Believers as well. Through books, tapes, and satellite television, we can now identify with believers from other parts of the globe. Speakers can be flown in by jet to conferences where the cross-fertilization of ideas and networking of relationships take place. (I believe that God inspired the genius for these information systems not to market worldly commodities, but to share communication between believers in different parts of the world and to spread the gospel.)

The Mystery of the Church

If there is to be a message from God to the Church as one body, that message must involve the unity of the people who are to receive it. The message *to* the Church is a vision *for* the Church. God has a glorious purpose and role for the Church in these endtimes.

> *And to make all see what is the fellowship of the mystery, which from the beginning of the ages has been hidden in God who created all things through Jesus Christ; to the intent that now the manifold wisdom of God might be made known by the church to the principalities and powers in the heavenly places.*
>
> Ephesians 3:9-10

The Scriptures refer to God's purposes for the Church as a mystery. A spiritual revelation is required in order to understand what that purpose is. The fellowship and unity emerging in the Church of our day is part of the predestined plan of God. The Church is to be an example in this present age for what God desires in the age to come.

Modeling Reconciliation

As sin caused a breakdown in mankind's relationship with God, it also caused a breakdown in the relationships between man and man (see Gen. 3–4). The gospel reconciles us to God, but through the cross we are also to be reconciled to one another. As God has forgiven us, so are we to forgive one another (see Mt. 6:12-15).

A sinful world is necessarily fraught with division and betrayal. As Joseph Garlington has stated, "In a divided world, only the Church can model reconciliation." The testimony of love and unity among believers is one of the most significant evidences for the truth of the gospel.

Just as there will be a one-world movement in the secular world, so there will be a trend toward unity in the Body of Christ. However, these two systems stand in opposition to one another. In God's view, only two societies, or philosophical systems, exist in the earth. One is the world; the other is the Church.

The Difference Between Earth and World

We should note that the words *world* and *earth* usually designate two completely different concepts in the Scriptures. The *earth* is the material planet created by God. It is essentially positive in that it was created by God's design. However, the present state of the earth exists in a corrupted and defiled form.

For the creation was subjected to futility, not willingly, but because of Him who subjected it in hope; because the creation itself also will be delivered from the bondage of corruption into the glorious liberty of the children of God.

Romans 8:20-21

The earth is also equivalent to what people refer to as *nature*. Natural creation has been adversely affected by the fall of man and by our continuing sin. As God's plan is completed, and as redeemed people gain control of the earth, natural creation will be restored to a paradise-like condition.

But the meek shall inherit the earth.

Psalm 37:11a

There is nothing in the earth, materially speaking, that we cannot receive and enjoy as long as we do so with a proper attitude of thanksgiving and holiness (see 1 Tim. 4:4). [1]

Not understanding the difference between the world and the earth has caused believers to overestimate Satan's influence and authority. Satan is referred to as the "god of this world" (2 Cor. 4:4 KJV), which means he is

---

1. The problem is not with things, but in people's attitude toward things. There is nothing inherently wrong with sex, food, money, power, and sleep; it is the perversions of lust, gluttony, greed, ambition, and laziness that ruin our attitude toward material things. When our psychological attachment to things becomes greater than our love for God, we have fallen into the slavery of sin (see 1 Cor. 6:12).

the leader of sinful people and of rebellious angels who fell under his sway.

The *world*, on the other hand, is not a natural creation. It is the gathered folkways of the sinful population of the earth; the sum total of the selfish desires of mankind. It also may be seen as the universal negative peer pressure among human beings of all ages.

Dominion in the Earth

Satan is not God; nor is he Lord. The fact that he is the god of the present evil world system does not mean that he has legitimate authority or rights over the planet. On the contrary, his influence is established through evil-hearted people. He is an outlaw. Any authority he exercises on the earth is illegal and illegitimate.

The earth is the Lord's, and all its fullness....
Psalm 24:1

This planet belongs to God and God's people. We should not relinquish any aspect of the earth or its resources to the forces of evil. We should not yield any area of governmental authority to the devil by mistakenly thinking it is his rightful domain. Nothing is the rightful domain of the devil other than the people who have chosen to serve him.

The Church may be seen as the vanguard of God's forces reasserting His claim to this planet. In God's eyes we are not strangers and outcasts in the earth. Rather, as children of God, we are heirs of all that He has created (see Rom. 8:17). God calls us to occupy this territory as His appointed stewards until He returns (see Lk. 19:13 KJV). We will be held accountable for the degree we worked for an increase in the spiritual and material prosperity of the planet (see Mt. 25:20-30).

The dominion of God's people includes dominion over the financial resources of the earth. Gold itself as a natural creation is good (see Gen. 2:12). God has always maintained that the gold and silver belong to Him (see Hag. 2:8). The Law of Moses asserts that all of the real estate belongs to God as well (see Lev. 25:23a).

We are strangers and pilgrims in this world in two senses. First, we understand that God is the ultimate owner of everything. Thus we are heirs and stewards in a delegated manner, secondary to His absolute sovereignty (see Lev. 25:23b). We are temporarily pilgrims in a world that belongs permanently to God. Second, our experience in this life is one of being an outcast or a sojourner because a sinful world rejects godly people (see Heb. 11:13). Because much injustice takes place in the world, selfish people are often found in control of the means and ways of temporal power.

The Battle Between the World and the Church

This world system of injustice is being brought to an end (see 1 Cor. 2:6). Jesus is already reigning at the right hand of the Father. He is the Lord of lords right now. He is the ultimate governor of the planet. Satan may be seen as the leader of a large pocket of rebellion, but he is not the governor. Jesus is in the process of crushing that rebellion. We, as His Church, are the representatives of His government on this earth (see 2 Cor. 5:20).[2]

The world and the Church are in conflict; they clash with one another on the earth. A battle is going on between the forces loyal to Jesus and the forces loyal to Satan. That battle takes place both on the earth and in the spiritual realm surrounding the earth, involving both humans and angels.

The battle between the world and the Church is growing more intense as the end of this age draws near. The Book of Revelation describes the culmination of the battle between good and evil. That battle has always been here, but rises to a crescendo and reaches a climax shortly before the return of the Messiah. This intensifying of spiritual warfare is the best perspective from which to interpret the Book of Revelation.

God's Judgment and Wrath

Three factors contribute to the cataclysmic events described in the Book of Revelation. The first is this: *God is*

---

2. The world is the corporate race of fallen man. We are called to love the world in the sense that we love the people who are in the world. God loves the people in the world so much that He gave His Son in order to save them out of the world (see Jn. 3:16). On the other hand, we are called to hate and separate ourselves from all the lustful desires and selfish intentions in the world system (1 Jn. 2:15).

pouring out His wrath and judgment upon an ungodly and evil world. The wrath of God is a blessed thing, although it is horrible in the magnitude of its vengeance. God's judgment is an exercise of His justice. (*Justice* and *judgment* have the same Hebrew word: *mishpat*.)

> *Then the sky receded as a scroll when it is rolled up, and every mountain and island was moved out of its place. And the kings of the earth...and every free man, hid themselves in the caves and in the rocks of the mountains, and said to the mountains and rocks, "Fall on us and hide us from the face of Him who sits on the throne and from the wrath of the Lamb! For the great day of His wrath has come, and who is able to stand?"*
>
> Revelation 6:14-17

These punishments actually are a cause for rejoicing! They are righteous. We should rejoice in the same way we rejoice when a hardened criminal is brought to justice or a mass murderer is caught and executed.

There are two types of judgment from God. The first is a *disciplinary* judgment that God brings upon His people to purge them and cleanse them of evil desires. These disciplinary judgments are not destructive but corrective. They are of a different nature than the harsher judgments brought upon the world. They are as different as a spanking is from a case of lung cancer.

The second type of judgment from God is *punitive*. The plagues in the Book of Revelation are similar to the plagues in the book of Exodus. In Exodus God's purpose was to destroy an evil society on which He has already pronounced judgment. These punitive judgments give God glory in the sense that they demonstrate that God is more powerful than the evil found in the world. The punitive judgments are also executed in the hope that people will turn from their evil ways. However, more often than not, evil people react by being further hardened in their resentment.

> *And men were scorched with great heat, and they blasphemed the name of God who has power over these plagues; and they did not repent and give Him glory.*
> Revelation 16:9

God causes the trumpet judgments and plagues of the Book of Revelation as an expression of His wrath and justice. The Bible states that the process of judgment begins first with the disciplinary correction of God toward His own people (see 1 Pet. 4:17). Then the process of judgment moves to the second stage of punitive destruction against those who are in rebellion to God.

Persecution of the Saints

The second factor that causes the terrible events of the Book of Revelation is this: *The people of this world and the forces of Satan persecute the people of God in their spite against God.* Since the Church is God's representative body upon the earth, Satan has always desired to afflict believers and attack them (as well as tempt them with pride and lust). In the endtimes, as the battle increases between good and evil, so will the persecution and attacks against the saints intensify.

> *It was granted to him* [the Beast] *to make war with the saints and to overcome them...and cause as many as would not worship the image of the beast to be killed.*
> Revelation 13:7,15

Difficult times are coming for the saints (that is, believers) who are alive in the final years before the return of Jesus. However, their tribulations do not come from God, but from those who hate God. God does not pour out His wrath (punitive judgment) upon His children. Trials and temptations do not come upon the saints from God (see Jas. 1:13).

> *For God did not appoint us to wrath, but to obtain salvation through our Lord Jesus Christ.*
> 1 Thessalonians 5:9

It is not God who orchestrates the persecution of the saints. God is on our side. He is working toward our salvation, not our destruction. The attacks that come upon the people of God are carried out by the forces of Satan and his followers. The disastrous events and tribulations of the endtimes are caused by two entirely different sources. On the one hand God is punishing evil; on the other hand a sinful world is persecuting the saints.

God does, however, lead His people to confront evil. He also uses difficulties to chasten and correct us. So we do not want to avoid the disciplinary measures of God (see Heb. 12:5-11). God will direct us into greater and greater battles as our faith to handle those situations grows. Often what is most uncomfortable to us is a challenge God wants us to face for the greater good of His Kingdom (see Mt. 26:37-39).

Protection for the Saints

The third factor of the end-times battle is, *God provides supernatural protection for His people upon the earth.* It is essential that God's people know they can find refuge and security in the Lord. He is able to protect us in the worst of situations; He is able to provide for us even when the world is falling apart.

It is not my purpose here to argue for one kind of eschatology or another. Whether you are pre-trib, post-trib, post-mil, or a-mil, you still need to be able to walk in the supernatural power and protection of the Holy Spirit. The world is already falling apart. Although the world situation will become immeasurably worse in the decades to come, there is already a degree in which God's judgment is being executed upon the ungodly, and in which the world system is persecuting the saints. God's Word promises us victory no matter how bad circumstances are.

Yet in all these things we are more than conquerors through Him who loved us.
                                                            Romans 8:37

"All these things," in which we are "more than conquerors," includes tribulation, persecution, being led to the slaughter, the sword, etc. (Rom. 8:35-39). We, the Church, need to gain a victorious and faith-filled understanding of our own role if we are to deal with the spiritual warfare that confronts us.

The Exodus Example

In the Book of Exodus, while the ten plagues fell upon Egypt and their pagan deities, the Israelites were supernaturally protected.

And in that day I will set apart the land of Goshen, in which My people dwell, that no swarms of flies shall be there, in order that you may know that I am the Lord in the midst of the land.

Exodus 8:22

"And the Lord will make a difference between the livestock of Israel and the livestock of Egypt...." So the Lord did this thing on the next day, and all the livestock of Egypt died; but of the livestock of the children of Israel, not one died.

Exodus 9:4-6

Only in the land of Goshen, where the children of Israel were, there was no hail.

Exodus 9:26

The Five Streams

> *...and there was thick darkness in all the land of Egypt three days. They did not see one another; nor did anyone rise from his place for three days. But all the children of Israel had light in their dwellings.*
>
> Exodus 10:22-23

What awesome miracles! The supernatural protection of God's people in the face of God's judgment upon evil gives glory to His name. God desires to make a distinction between His people and the people of the world.

Sealed for Protection

The Book of Revelation also describes supernatural protection for the saints of God.

> *..."Do not harm the earth, the sea, or the trees till we have sealed the servants of our God on their foreheads."*
>
> Revelation 7:3

God can provide for us and even prosper us in the midst of famine and economic collapse (see Gen. 26:1,12; Ps. 37:19). If the Church can have the faith that when we lay hands on people afflicted with AIDS, they will recover (see Mk. 16:18), then we at least need to have the faith that we ourselves will not be destroyed. God has sent His angels to surround us and protect us.

> *A thousand may fall at your side, and ten thousand at your right hand; but it shall not come near you. ... No*

evil shall befall you, nor shall any plague come near your dwelling; for He shall give His angels charge over you, to keep you in all your ways.
Psalm 91:7,10-11

In the endtimes there will be no middle ground. The world will become more and more evil as the Church will become more and more pure. There will be no compromise. Thus the clash will continue until there is no possible resolution other than utter destruction of the one side or the other.

That last battle in which one side or the other will be destroyed is referred to as Armageddon. Armageddon is the culmination of the conflict between the world and the Church. It is at that time that Jesus will return at the head of an angelic army to destroy the forces of evil (see Joel 3; Zech. 14; Rev. 19).

Wrath and Mercy

Wrath and mercy are both part of God's character. God extends His mercy to all; any who accept His mercy become vessels of mercy and honor (see Rom. 9:23; 2 Tim. 2:20). Those who reject His mercy receive His wrath.

> *…"The hand of our God is upon all those for good who seek Him, but His power and His wrath are against all those who forsake Him."*
> Ezra 8:22

In the endtimes, God's wrath will be poured out in a terrible way upon those who refuse to believe. At the same time, His mercy will be poured out in a wonderful way to those who stand in faith. God's grace has been extended to humanity through Jesus. If a person rejects Jesus, he has nothing left but the wrath of God.

He who believes in the Son has everlasting life; and he who does not believe the Son shall not see life, but the wrath of God abides on him.

John 3:36

Wrath or mercy—it's our choice. God prefers us to be a vessel of mercy. If we remove from our hearts the kind of sinful and treacherous attitudes that God hates, then we will be vessels of mercy. On the other hand, if we choose to cling to evil, we will be vessels of wrath.

But in a great house there are not only vessels of gold and silver, but also of wood and clay, some for honor and some for dishonor. Therefore if anyone cleanses himself from the latter, he will be a vessel for honor, sanctified and useful for the Master, prepared for every good work.

2 Timothy 2:20-21

God's wrath is poured out on evil. Unbelievers who are submitted to evil receive the total wrath of God. Also, believers who cling to pockets of evil in their lives will have a purging or disciplinary wrath directed at that area of evil.

The wrath of God is simply part of His just nature. Thus the saints of God praise God for His justice; we rejoice when His wrath is poured out on evil (see Rev. 18:20).

A Victorious Eschatology

Are we to have a "doom and gloom" attitude concerning end-times prophecies? Certainly the picture for an unbelieving world is horribly gloomy. Sinners are facing the wrath of God in temporal plagues and eternal damnation. We, though, are not of the world.

It is true the world is doomed. Therefore we must emphasize their need for salvation from that doom. The saints, on the other hand, have been removed from the world system by a radical change of heart. We are being trained in the Spirit for a glorious destiny. There is no reason for us to have a defeatist attitude toward the endtimes.

> *...the world has hated them because they are not of the world, just as I am not of the world.*
> John 17:14

Yes, the world hates us and persecutes us. But our destiny is not the same as theirs. No matter how horrible the battle becomes, the ultimate outcome is assured: *we win*. Although we need to purge our hearts of every worldly lust and desire so we will not be punished with the world, our ultimate destiny is not in hell but in Heaven.

My brethren, count it all joy when you fall into various trials.
                                             James 1:2

Even when the world, the flesh, and the devil attack us, we know that our joyful victory is assured through Jesus. Even if they kill our bodies, we will still be resurrected to eternal glory and dominion (see Lk. 12:4).

God does not lead us to run away from the attacks of the world, but to maintain a moral purity and a victorious attitude in the midst of those attacks.

I do not pray that You should take them out of the world, but that You should keep them from the evil one.
                                             John 17:15

There is no doubt that the world is an evil place in which to live. Unfortunately, the world will become darker and darker with every passing day. That is a sobering truth, but it is not a cause for alarm or a desire to escape within us. Rather the darkness of this world is an opportunity for us to be greater witnesses for the light of Jesus.

That you may become blameless and harmless, children of God without fault in the midst of a crooked and perverse generation, among whom you shine as lights in the world.
                                        Philippians 2:15

We, as the saints of God, need to warn the world of the horrible judgment and wrath that is coming upon them. We need to gird our loins to stand victorious in faith in the midst of persecution. We need to undergo the disciplines of God so we are purged of every worldly desire.

A Pure and Glorious Bride

In the midst of these difficulties, we must maintain a positive vision of God's glorious destiny for the Church. The Church is to be both pure and powerful in the endtimes. The world may be a sinking ship, but we are a glorious Bride being prepared for her Husband (Jesus).

That He might present her to Himself a glorious church, not having spot or wrinkle or any such thing, but that she should be holy and without blemish.
Ephesians 5:27

This is Jesus' view of the Church. Despite all our mistakes, He brings us to purity and victory. According to the Bible, victory is based on moral purity. Thus the Church is glorious because it is without spot or wrinkle. Even the very word *saints* means those who are being made holy (see Heb. 12:23). Our victory over the devil is in repenting of sins, receiving forgiveness in the blood of Jesus, and so by faith rising above the enemy's attempts to defile us and condemn us (see Col. 2:14; 1 Jn. 1:7-9; Rev. 7:14; 12:10-11).

The endtimes are not only a time of evil in the world, but also a time in which the Church, as Jesus' Bride, is making herself ready.

The Five Streams

> *...for the marriage of the Lamb has come, and His wife has made herself ready.*
>
> Revelation 19:7

The Church that Jesus is coming back for is one that has already been made ready. Jesus is not coming back for an immature bride. This, then, is our view of the Church. Our evaluation is not according to the standards or measurements of the world, not dampened by the negativity of the world around us. Instead our positive view of the Church stems from our relationship with Jesus and the fact that we are being prepared to be His Bride!

Chapter 2

Unity Brings Revival

The unity of the Church is necessary for revival. We all want revival, but God wants revival even more than we do. We do not have to try to persuade God to bring revival. He is already predisposed to do so.

However, revivals do not happen by accident. God does not pour out His Spirit on a whim. Actually, it is our prayer for revival that primarily changes us. Since God is already predisposed to give revival, the issue is merely one of bringing people to a condition of receptivity.

God is not a respecter of persons (see Acts 10:34 KJV). He will pour out His Spirit on any individual who will receive Him. A revival is when the Holy Spirit is poured out on a large number of people together.

There is one body and one Spirit, just as you were called in one hope of your calling.

Ephesians 4:4

But one and the same Spirit works all these things, distributing to each one individually as He wills.
                                               1 Corinthians 12:11

There is only one Holy Spirit. If we are to receive the outpouring of the Spirit together, we must have unity of heart. The early Church was born in the midst of an outpouring of the Holy Spirit during the holy day of Shavuot (Pentecost). That wonderful revival is a pattern for the rest of the Church to follow.

Unified Prayer at Pentecost

What was it that put those early believers in a position to receive such an outpouring? There were several factors. First, they had spent almost three years with Jesus; they had just witnessed His resurrection and had been instructed by Him after the resurrection. Also, the entire area had been prepared for revival by the ministry of John the Baptist and Jesus. Finally, it was a historical moment appointed by God for the birth of the Church. It also seems clear, since Peter quoted passages from Joel, that Jesus' followers had been meditating on Scriptures dealing with revival.

However, there was yet another factor that had much to do with their receptivity to the outpouring of the Holy Spirit.

When the Day of Pentecost had fully come, they were all with one accord in one place. And suddenly there came

a sound from heaven, as of a rushing mighty wind, and it filled the whole house where they were sitting.
                                       Acts 2:1-2

What was the condition of the believers immediately before they received the Holy Spirit? They were "all with one accord in one place." That is a clear description of unity and harmony. The Holy Spirit cannot be poured out in revival upon people who are in strife. Unity and love among believers is a crucial prerequisite for revival.

Not only were the believers in one accord, but they also were doing something in the midst of that harmony.

These all continued with one accord in prayer and supplication....
                                       Acts 1:14

What were they doing when in one accord and one place? They were praying. By the example of Acts 1 and 2, we may conclude that unified prayer—praying together in unity—is the key to revival. The combination of prayer and unity allows for the spark of revival to catch.

That the World May Know

When Jesus prayed for the unity of the believers (see Jn. 17), He indicated that the oneness of the believers would cause other people to come to know the Lord.

> *That they all may be one, as You, Father, are in Me, and I in You; that they also may be one in Us, that the world may believe that You sent Me.*
>
> John 17:21

When we demonstrate our union with God and our unity with one another, the world will believe in Jesus. Unfortunately, history has demonstrated a reverse of this text. The world has not seen us manifesting our oneness with God nor unity with one another. Consequently, they have not come to believe our message about Jesus.

> *...that they may be made perfect in one, and that the world may know that You have sent Me, and have loved them as You have loved Me.*
>
> John 17:23

We see the same pattern: first union with God and unity in the Church, then evangelism to the world. The world will not see a sweep of evangelism until the Church first comes to a place of unity. When we come to unity, a new tide of revival will be released.

First Be Reconciled

Oh, how we want to see revival and an outpouring of the Holy Spirit! Sometimes we want to see a manifestation of the power of God so much that we do not spend time on our relationships with one another. We are too wrapped up in ministering under our own anointing to listen to what God has to say through someone else.

Ironically, the more we seek to lay hold of the anointing in a sectarian or separatist way, the more we actually push the Spirit of revival further away from us. God views the outpouring of His Spirit as integrally connected with loving relationships among His people. The discussion of the charismatic gifts in First Corinthians 12 is interwoven with the description of the believers as members of a single body. That great passage on divine love, First Corinthians 13, is nestled between the discussion of the gifts of the Spirit in chapters 12 and 14.

I repeat, God links the outpouring of His Spirit to unity among His people. Our relationship with God is more important than our relationship with one another, but God makes us deal with our problems with other people before we continue in our relationship with Him.

> *Therefore if you bring your gift to the altar, and then remember that your brother has something against you, leave your gift there before the altar, and go your way. First be reconciled to your brother, and then come and offer your gift.*
>
> Matthew 5:23-24

Reconciliation with others is a prerequisite to worship. Personally, I would rather seek the face of God than deal with issues of reconciliation with other people. But God has determined that if we are to experience His presence in worship, we must first come to a place of reconciliation with one another.

Laying Down Our Lives for the Church

Those who desire revival are being directed by God to give attention to the unity of the Church. So even though we focus on unity, our real goal is revival. We seek the Kingdom of God. But if we are to experience the presence of God in a much greater dimension, we must give ourselves to serving the unity of the Church.

> *...just as Christ also loved the church and gave Himself for her.*
>
> Ephesians 5:25

Jesus laid down His life for the Church—we are to do the same. His willingness to lay down His life stemmed from the joy that He had over the vision of the Church becoming His Bride (see Heb. 12:2). As Jesus gave Himself for the Church, salvation and eternal life were released to mankind. Likewise, as we give ourselves to the unity and purity of the Church, revival and evangelism will be released.

Cooperative Prayer Meetings

It would seem rather simple to gather people of different streams in the Body of Christ to pray for revival. However, that simple step requires a great deal of faith. First of all, we in each stream must stop seeing other churches and ministries as our competition, let alone our opposition. We need to exercise "faith working through love" (Gal. 5:6) in order to trust people who previously hurt us or whom we considered untrustworthy.

Many people have been participating in cooperative prayer meetings. (Francis Frangipane has done an excellent job the past few years in promoting this vision in many cities throughout the country.) Charismatic, pentecostal, evangelical, fundamental, denominational, and nondenominational groups are coming together to pray for revival.

For those of us who are used to *feeling* the anointing, community-wide, joint prayer meetings may not feel very anointed. We are not used to praying with those of a different spiritual or denominational background, so we feel uncomfortable. Of course, feelings of comfort are not the best barometer with which to measure the purposes of God.

We must humble ourselves to submit to something that, at first, may not seem spiritual or exciting. We set aside personal goals of ministry in order to further the greater purposes of the Kingdom of God. Submitting to one another for the unity of the Church is a proving ground for the humility upon which God will later pour out His Spirit in powerful signs and wonders. It is a test of character to discern the move and purposes of God in events that do not feel comfortable or stimulating. Spirituality is not always sensational or spectacular; after all, we walk by faith and not by sight (see 2 Cor. 5:7).

Unity as Spiritual Warfare

When we speak of praying for revival, we necessarily deal with the topic of spiritual warfare. Certainly, Satan and his forces do not want a revival to take place in our midst. It follows, then, that if we work for revival, we are sure to encounter demonic opposition. Since the unity of the Church is a prerequisite for spiritual revival, the attacks of the enemy are often focused on causing division among us. If Satan can cause division, he has won that battle. If he can cause division, he can hinder revival from springing up in our midst.

..."Every kingdom divided against itself is brought to desolation, and a house divided against a house falls. If Satan also is divided against himself, how will his kingdom stand?..."

Luke 11:17-18

"Divide and conquer" is the most basic rule of warfare, both spiritual and natural. The rule works both ways; it is true for both sides. Whichever side is divided will fall, and whichever side remains united will stand.

If we can divide the forces of Satan, they will fall. If the devil can divide us, we will fall. If we can maintain our unity, we will stand. The effort to maintain our unity is, in effect, a spiritual battle against the devil.

For we do not wrestle against flesh and blood, but against principalities, against powers, against the rulers of the darkness of this age, against spiritual hosts of wickedness in the heavenly places.

Ephesians 6:12

Our battle is not against other people, even though it seems to be that way. The breakdown of interpersonal relationships between believers is evidence of an attack from demonic forces. When we win back a brother in reconciliation, or when we enter a new stage of unity in the Church, we can assume that there has been a victory somewhere in the warfare between angels and demons.

Unity Brings Revival

Our effort to serve the unity of the Church is an act of spiritual warfare. When we submit humbly to one another in love, we aggressively launch an attack against the devil.

Therefore submit to God. Resist the devil and he will flee from you. ... Humble yourselves in the sight of the Lord, and He will lift you up.

James 4:7,10

When we humble ourselves before the Lord, we wage war against the devil. That humility often takes the form of submitting to one another. Giving up our personal agendas and ambitions for the sake of the greater unity of the Body of Christ is a courageous act of aggression against demonic forces.

When we seek the unity of the Church, we are often forced to deal with frustrating relationships. Those frustrations are another evidence that we are in the midst of a spiritual battle. Thus every time we can withstand the disappointments of interpersonal relationships and maintain the unity of the brethren, we have won a mighty victory in the spiritual realm.

Endeavoring to keep the unity of the Spirit in the bond of peace.

Ephesians 4:3

As mentioned before, the unity of the Church is required for revival. But this unity will not just happen. On the contrary, believers must seek it with determination, and by spiritual warfare in the heavenlies.

Praying for Jerusalem

We know that Jesus is now at the right hand of the Father interceding for us (see Heb. 7:25, Rom. 8:34). He intercedes for us for many things. In John 17, one of the main themes of His prayer for us is our unity. Jesus prayed in a similar way when He interceded for the city of Jerusalem.

O Jerusalem, Jerusalem, the one who kills the prophets and stones those who are sent to her! How often I wanted to gather your children together, as a hen gathers her chicks under her wings, but you were not willing!
Matthew 23:37

Jesus' prayer here has spiritual applications on several levels. As He prayed for Jerusalem, so may we pray for revival in whatever city we live. Jesus prayed for the city as a unit. He had a heart for the spiritual welfare and revival among the population of the city as a whole.

If this prayer may be applied to any city in the world, how much more so may it be applied directly to the city of Jerusalem itself today. Unified prayer for any city is a key to revival. Unified prayer for Jerusalem is essential not only for a revival there, but also as an element affecting the Second Coming (see Mt. 23:39).

Notice the phrase "gather your children together." The unbelievers are gathered out of the world into salvation under the wings of the Messiah. In addition, the language here of "gathering together" seems to speak especially to the issue of unity. Jesus prays not only for the lost to be saved, but also for the believers in the city to come into unity.

If we are to cooperate with Jesus' present ministry of intercessory prayer, we should involve ourselves in praying for the unity of the believers in whatever city we may live. Christians everywhere can also have a part in interceding for the unity of the Jewish believers in Jerusalem. In this way we pray for the peace of Jerusalem (see Ps. 122:6).

The unity of the believers in Jerusalem is a significant battlefront of spiritual warfare in the endtimes.

The Samson Cycle

The story of Samson (Judg. 13-16) has symbolic parallels to the dilemma of the modern Church in America. Samson had an early dedication to the Lord in his youth. His life had been consecrated to the Lord by his parents. This is similar to the role of the pilgrims and founding fathers in the history of the Church in America. There was a pure dedication and a desire for holiness among the early settlers that preceded the American Church of today. Our forefathers had a long-range vision that their children and children's children would serve the Lord and make America a country dedicated to God.

Over the past 300 years the American Church has seen times of great strength and anointing. So it was in the life of Samson—he experienced an anointing of power in his young life.

Unfortunately, as Samson grew older he began to take his anointing for granted. He compromised on moral issues, particularly with women. Likewise today we have seen a certain degree of moral compromise in the

The Five Streams

Church in America—a lukewarmness on issues of holiness, and a problem of immorality within the ministry.

Samson violated the principle that his anointing was conditional, that it depended on his being faithful to his oath of consecration. (The secret of Samson's strength was not his hair, but holiness. His hair was a symbol of his covenant with God to walk in holiness, with no compromise to worldly standards.) Because Samson violated the conditions of his Nazarite vow, he fell into defeat, humiliation, and weakness. Today the American Church has suffered humiliation at the hands of the secular press (the Philistines of our day) because of our sins of immorality. We have also suffered a period of weakness in which many of the miraculous signs and wonders so prevalent in mass evangelism in Third World countries have been lacking in our midst.

A New Consecration

The Philistines, Samson's enemies, did not notice that during his period of humiliation, Samson was searching his heart to reconsider his consecration to God. While they laughed at his weakened state, a new strength born out of humility and rededication was growing within him. In America today, while the secular world mocks the Church, many of the ministers are going through a period of soul searching and rededication. The more the world has been laughing, the more the Church has been reconsidering her foundation of holiness. What the devil meant to humiliate us, has been used by God to humble us.

Many ministers are letting go of soulish ambitions and agendas out of that humility. A quiet, desperate desire to do whatever is necessary to see revival is growing. Pastors are seeking one another out to pray for the good of the community around them. The outward humiliation of the American Church has served, in some quarters, to develop a new vision for the unity of the Body of Christ.

The story of Samson concludes with a return of the anointing and a dedication in which he gives up his life for the Kingdom of God. Great victory is won in a short period of time. So I believe it is God's desire for the Church in America to return to a place of power and anointing, that a mighty harvest of souls may then be reaped as in the rapid stroke of a sickle.

Purity and Power

The Church in America today has a choice. If we continue in compromise and complacency, we will never rise out of our present state of impotency. On the other hand, if a new zeal and consecration arises in us, anointing and revival power are sure to follow. If that happens, we will see the power structures of the Philistine establishment come crashing down around us. The political forces representing humanism and ungodliness will fall.

The biblical principle is this: purity precedes power. God desires both purity and power in His people. Even Jesus was strong and gentle. So in His personality we see the full expression of purity and power. Holiness and faith go together. One without the other is just a form of phony religion (2 Tim. 3:5).

The power of God is available to produce purity within us; the Holy Spirit is the spirit of holiness. So we cannot become pure unless we have the power of God. Thus the biblical principle is also this: power precedes purity. If you want to be holy, you must receive the power of the Holy Spirit. You must have the power to walk in purity. You also need have purity to walk in power. Do not settle for one without the other. In fact, it is impossible to have one without the other.

Racial Reconciliation and Revival

Unity is necessary to produce revival because of the issue of racial reconciliation as well. Any manifestation of the Kingdom of God in a local area must include reconciliation of the major racial groups in that area.

For He Himself is our peace, who has made both one, and has broken down the middle wall of separation, having abolished in His flesh the enmity, that is, the law of commandments contained in ordinances, so as to create in Himself one new man from the two, thus making peace, and that He might reconcile them both to God in one body through the cross, thereby putting to death the enmity.

Ephesians 2:14-16

Unity Brings Revival

In the early Church the primary racial issue needing resolved was between Jew and Gentile (this disagreement runs throughout the Book of Acts). Later the issue became one of Romans versus non-Romans. The gospel demands that racial groups come together in unity.

In America the most predominant racial issue in inner cities is Black and White relations. No real spiritual peace can be brought to our cities without encompassing some solution to the hatred and mistrust that exists between many Blacks and Whites.

Only the gospel has the power to deliver someone from the roots of racism. Only the gospel can cause Blacks and Whites to love one another and come together as one body. Thus the gospel must be preached in our cities with an application and relevancy to racial problems. No matter how much a Black person may have hated or mistrusted Whites, when he is born again, he can love his neighbor through the Spirit of God. The same is true for a White person. Through the Spirit of God, he can be free from any desire to separate himself from his Black neighbor.

Tikkun Ministries' program for racial reconciliation in our cities rests squarely with the gospel. Both Blacks and Whites need to be transformed by the power of faith in Jesus so they can then love one another. Then they can come together within the community of the Body of Christ and demonstrate their mutual reconciliation before the world. That testimony of reconciliation will release a mighty wave of revival throughout our cities.

The Five Streams

Racial reconciliation is an important facet of the overall unity of the Church, and a key factor to releasing revival in our cities.

Jewish and Arab Reconciliation

As Black and White reconciliation is a key to releasing revival power in the cities of America, so is Jew and Arab reconciliation a key to releasing revival in Jerusalem, Judea, and Samaria (the West Bank), and the rest of the Middle East.

Tikkun Ministries' program for racial reconciliation in that area of the world is similar to the one in America. It brings the Arabs to a saving knowledge of Jesus the Messiah. It also brings the Jews to a saving knowledge of Jesus the Messiah. Then it teaches them to love one another through the power of God's Spirit and to demonstrate the testimony of mutual reconciliation to the world around them. That testimony of reconciliation then releases a powerful revival that will spread throughout the Middle East.

The problem with Jew and Arab reconciliation is the depth of the division between them. It is deeper than with any other racial problem in history. Without minimizing the difficulties between Blacks and Whites in America, their racial problems have existed for only 300 years. Those roots are relatively shallow when compared to the 3,000-year history of animosity between the Jew and Arab. (See also Amos 1:11; Obadiah 10.)

Unity Brings Revival

So Esau hated Jacob because of the blessing with which his father blessed him....
Genesis 27:41

Because you have had an ancient hatred, and have shed the blood of the children of Israel by the power of the sword at the time of their calamity....
Ezekiel 35:5

Today tensions in the Middle East constantly threaten international military confrontation. Those tensions are more of a spiritual origin than a political one. Although the misperceptions and racial barriers between Jews and Arabs are quite deep, they can be conquered through the power of the gospel. Outreaches have already begun among both the Arabs and the Jews. A vision for the ministry of reconciliation between Jew and Arab is also beginning.

In that day Israel will be one of three with Egypt and Assyria—a blessing in the midst of the land.
Isaiah 19:24

There are promises in the Bible, such as this one in Isaiah, that reconciliation will take place between Jew and Arab no matter how insurmountable the obstacles may seem.

The Parable of Jacob and Esau

I believe the Lord will use the tensions between the Jews and the Arabs to bring them to a point of receptivity

The Five Streams

to the gospel. Both Orthodox Judaism and Islam have set themselves in opposition to the gospel; however, neither is able to solve the racial problems between the Jews and the Arabs.

It is partly through their inability to solve the conflict with the Arabs that the Jews will turn in desperation to Jesus. For the Arabs, their willingness to recognize God's calling upon the Jews is what will free them to see Jesus as their Messiah. This dynamic can be seen symbolically in the story of the reconciliation between Jacob and Esau found in Genesis 32–33.

The story takes place when Jacob returns to the Promised Land after a prolonged sojourn out of the country. As he returns, he is forced to deal with the conflict with his brother Esau that has lain dormant all those years. Likewise, Jews today find themselves dealing with the conflict with the Arabs as they return to Israel after many years in the diaspora. The ancient enmity between the Jews and Arabs has resurfaced as a modern political issue.

When Jacob is forced to face his brother Esau, he cries out in desperation to God and wrestles all night with a divine figure in the form of a man. After wrestling, the Man touches Jacob's thigh and changes his name to Israel. Similarly, the Jews will wrestle spiritually with their inability to be reconciled with their Arab neighbors until they cry out in desperation to God. In that wrestling they will encounter the Man who will transform them from the Jacob identity to the Israel identity, and bring them into the spiritual land of promised salvation.

After struggling with this issue of reconciliation, Jacob says this to his brother Esau:

And Jacob said, "No, please, if I have now found favor in your sight, then receive my present from my hand, inasmuch as I have seen your face as though I had seen the face of God, and you were pleased with me."
Genesis 33:10

There was something about the impossibility of being reconciled to Esau that caused Jacob to have a revelation of God through the face of his brother Esau. Only God will be able to effect reconciliation between Jew and Arab in the Middle East. (He can and will do it, however.) Through their need to be utterly dependent on God, both Jew and Arab will come to a revelation of who God as they go through the difficult process of reconciliation.

The First Split

The split between Jew and Gentile was the first racial division in the Church. The struggle for reconciliation and mutual identity between Jew and Gentile pervades the New Testament writings. Just as it is the first split, it is also the most foundational. Since division causes weakness in the Body of Christ, the division between Jew and Gentile has hurt the Church deeply. As that division heals and a new dimension of mutual acceptance and understanding develops between Jewish and Gentile believers in Jesus, the Church will rise to a greater level of strength.

The split between Judaism and Christianity opened the door for Islam to win the hearts of the Arabs. By the early seventh century A.D., many Arabs were attracted to the biblical morality and monotheism found in the Judeo-Christian tradition. They were ripe for a harvest of salvation. Unfortunately, this divisiveness between Judaism and Christianity was a factor that encouraged Mohammed to develop his own synthesis of biblical revelation, with himself as the central prophetic figure.

It is also the reconciliation between Jew and Christian that holds the key to deliverance for the Arab peoples from the deception of Islam. If America and Israel can maintain themselves as allies, a basis strong enough to stop the fighting in the Middle East can be developed. If Jewish and Gentile believers in Jesus can demonstrate reconciliation, a significant spiritual barrier keeping the Arabs away from Jesus will be overcome. A Jewish and Gentile reconciliation in the Body of Christ would release an anointing for evangelism to the Arabs and revival in the Middle East.

Chapter 3

God's Answer to Alienation

The modern world is filled with every kind of convenience and contrivance that make people feel alienated. Alienation is the curse and overarching spiritual dilemma of our age.

The opposite of community, alienation is the syndrome by which every individual feels isolated. No one feels as if he really belongs anywhere. No one knows where he fits in. In an alienated society, the individual withdraws more and more into his bubble of isolation. He does not know how to communicate with his neighbor. He has virtually no one with whom to share intimate dialogue on a meaningful level.

Evidences of Alienation

How do we know our society is alienated? The nuclear family is falling apart. Friends are suddenly transferred to another part of the country by the companies they work for. People drive to work in their bubbles of steel and rubber and have no relationship with the other thousands of commuters around them.

Most of one's entertainment is found staring mindlessly at a video screen. The monologue of the television replaces after-dinner conversation and socializing with family members. A man's circle of friends now consists of an imaginary sphere of make-believe heroes and personalities fabricated by the media.

Embarrassing as it may seem, many men in America entertain the notion that their favorite movie star has fallen in love with them. They fancy themselves in all types of romantic interludes with their celluloid lover. Then they superimpose the fantasy of that love affair upon the woman to whom they are married. Their own marriage grows more and more mundane and disappointing as the years of media delusion roll by. His real-life wife can never live up to the immaculate and youthful beauty whom he watches on the screen and who is replaced every few years by Hollywood's newest starlet.

In an alienated world, every form of realistic intimate relationship is fractured. Man, who was made to be in relationship with others of his own kind, finds himself starving for fellowship. Loneliness pervades society like a dark shadow across the lives of millions who live virtually shoulder to shoulder in large metropolitan cities. Like someone on a lifeboat in the middle of an ocean, there is "water, water everywhere, but not a drop to drink." In the modern megalopolis, there are people,

people everywhere, but no one with whom to have an intimate friendship.

> *And the Lord God said, "It is not good that man should be alone...."*
> Genesis 2:18

God created man as a social being. We were not designed to live without fellowship. The paradigm of alienation in our modern world is indicative of a society that has completely divorced its infrastructure from the sense of community God originally intended.

The Gospel as an Invitation to Relationship

In this world of alienation, the Church is to offer a solution. We are to be a model community in which relationships can be restored. Out of the darkness of loneliness and alienation, people will run to find the light of fellowship with Jesus and His saints.

> *That which we have seen and heard we declare to you, that you also may have fellowship with us; and truly our fellowship is with the Father and with His Son Jesus Christ. ... But if we walk in the light as He is in the light, we have fellowship with one another....*
> 1 John 1:3,7

The message of the gospel is essentially an invitation into a relationship. The first disciples, who had a personal relationship with Jesus physically as well as spiritually,

The Five Streams

invited other people into their fellowship. It was not possible to even think of having a relationship with Jesus without entering into a relationship with the disciples. Consider this: We say today that people "get saved," but in the first century they said people were "added to the church" (see Acts 2:47).

To believe the gospel was to enter into relationship with the other people who had believed, and through them, into a relationship with Jesus. The message of the gospel is not primarily a doctrine to be affirmed, but a living relationship to be experienced. However, the method in which we preach the gospel often contradicts the very relational aspect of the gospel itself. Because most of us have grown up in an alienated society, we tend to pass on to unbelievers the informational content of the gospel message without offering them the relationship that goes with it.

We say to people, "Here, I am offering you a relationship," then we do not offer any relationship. Our actions make the message impossible to be believed. For someone to say on television, "Jesus loves you and I love you too," amounts to offering a relationship without being there to relate to the people. We hand someone a tract with a pretty picture on it, then we turn and run away because we are too embarrassed or uncomfortable with intimacy even to make eye contact with the person.

Ironically, we do have the intimate fellowship that people are looking for. The world is starving for just what we have to offer. They are running around frantically chasing after some carnal substitute for pure and intimate fellowship. People who do not realize they can find true male-and-female intimacy in marriage pursue sexual immorality. Others flock from one cult group or fad to another because they do not believe they can find a real spiritual encounter with God in the Church.

Friendship Evangelism

Polls on evangelism show that most people come to faith in Jesus through the friendship of a sincere Christian. Now, we should use every possible form of media evangelism, whether print, radio, or television. However, media evangelism can never replace the primary role of friendship evangelism. Since the gospel encounter is a relationship, it can be best propagated through a relationship.

Media evangelism sows seed in a broad way. Friendship evangelism is the hands-on work that usually harvests the souls. Passing out information about the gospel is similar to advertising. Establishing a friendship between a believer and an unbeliever is like the personal contact of the salesman who closes the sale.

What Is Church Life?

Many of our congregational functions and operations at Tikkun Ministries have been developed out of the techniques of an alienated society. We have programs where people can come in and watch a show as if they were in a theater. Then they go home without ever having to penetrate past a superficial level of relationship.

The Five Streams

Usually pastors and ministers operate their ministries with the techniques of modern business management. Many find it difficult to break out of their office routine to make relationships either with their own flock or with the unbelievers in the community around them.

> *And they continued steadfastly in the apostles' doctrine and fellowship, in the breaking of bread, and in prayers. ... So continuing daily with one accord in the temple, and breaking bread from house to house, they ate their food with gladness and simplicity of heart.*
>
> Acts 2:42,46

Here we have a picture of people regularly sharing their lives in intimate relationships. Other than preaching and prayer, their most common activity was eating meals together. Meeting in one another's homes for common meals and conversation was the central aspect of the social life of the early Christian communities. Those ever-widening circles of friendship describe the biblical pattern of what should be called *church life*.

It would be shocking to evaluate what percentage of our so-called church programs and activities reflect the pattern of the Book of Acts. (Ralph Neighbors has done an excellent evaluation in his book, *Where Do We Go From Here?*) Some of the elements we believe to be quite normal in Christian circles are not in the Bible. Now, that does not necessarily mean they are wrong; it should simply cause us to analyze what we are doing. There is virtually no mention of a weekly Sunday meeting, a church

God's Answer to Alienation

building, a pastor's office, a Sunday school, a Board of Trustees, and almost every other organizational format that we have developed as part of our Christian culture.

I am not against any of these elements. The problem comes when we get so wrapped up in programs patterned after an alienated society, that we leave no room for the cultivation of new circles of friends.

Heavenly Communities

The world is looking for true friendship. If our programs cause us to lose that vital aspect of church life, we have dropped the very thing that people around us are looking for. They want to have a real relationship with God—and they want to have real relationships with other people. The most precious thing about Heaven is not so much the streets of gold and the jeweled buildings, but the quality of loving relationships that we can experience with God, Jesus, and all the saints.

The world is dying for lack of a relationship with Jesus. They are also disoriented from a lack of any sense of community. In an alienated world, the Church is to be a model of heavenly community.

You are the light of the world. A city that is set on a hill cannot be hidden.
                                                    Matthew 5:14

Jesus is the light in the midst of the Church. We as a corporate body are to be a community of light to the

The Five Streams

world. We are a "city" shining with light. Love is light. Loving fellowship and relationships are light. Lack of love is darkness. Today a world of fractured relationships lives in darkness. Only the spirit of divine community within the Church offers light to our darkened and alienated planet.

Organism vs. Organization

If we, as a spiritual city, are to bring the light of fellowship into the world, we must recapture the vision of the Church as an expanding sphere of friendship circles. As John 15:2 suggests, we must prune away many of the Church programs that hinder interpersonal relationships. Since the Church is described as a "body," there is to be an organic linking together of its members like cells in a body.

> *From whom the whole body, joined and knit together by what every joint supplies, according to the effective working by which every part does its share, causes growth of the body for the edifying of itself in love.*
>
> Ephesians 4:16

If a local church does not foster intimate relationships between its members, it is not really a church at all; it simply is a meeting place. A Bible study should not be fashioned after a classroom, nor the worship service after a theater production. The pastor's job description

God's Answer to Alienation

should not be formed like a corporate executive's, nor the ministry of pastoral care after a psychologist's practice.

The spiritual stronghold of alienation gives everyone the impression that he is on the outside looking in. This principality of evil is aimed at keeping people away from feeling part of a Church community.

Accepted, Not Rejected

The spirit of alienation tells Blacks that Christianity is a White man's religion. It tells women that biblical faith is a form of oppression fabricated by male chauvinists. It tells men that faith in God is only for women and children. It tells children that religion is a boring activity only for adults. It tells sophisticated adults that faith is merely a naive fantasy for children. It tells the strong that religion is only for the weak who need a crutch. It tells the fallen that they are not good enough to meet God's standards. It tells the Jews that Christianity is a Gentile religion. It tells the Gentiles that Jesus is the Messiah only for the Jews. It tells singles that you have to be married to be part of the "in crowd" of the Church. It tells parents that they are too busy to have any time for Church activities.

...by which He made us accepted in the Beloved.

Ephesians 1:6

The truth is, there is a place for all of us in the Body of Messiah. We are all accepted by God. The lie of the devil is to make everyone feel rejected. If a person believes that the reason he feels rejected is the fault of Christians, he will begin to slip away from the congregational community and endanger his faith.

Whenever you have a thought such as "I am being rejected" or "No one loves me" or "I don't belong here," you should know immediately that the thought is not from God. We must train ourselves not to be conformed to the world's alienated way of thinking. We must learn not to react out of a sense of rejection. The congregational community should be a laboratory where we can be trained to accept and affirm one another. The Church is a model community where we learn to relate to other human beings on a deeper level. The Church is the breeding ground of reconciliation for disenfranchised people.

The Ministry of Reconciliation

In a divided world, only the Church can model reconciliation.

Now all things are of God, who has reconciled us to Himself through Jesus Christ, and has given us the ministry of reconciliation.
                                        2 Corinthians 5:18

We are messengers and agents of God's process of reconciliation. That reconciliation is first unto God, then unto one another.

God's Answer to Alienation

For He Himself is our peace, who has made both one, and has broken down the middle wall of separation...and that He might reconcile them both to God in one body through the cross....
                                                    Ephesians 2:14-16

The Church is to be a model of reconciliation in every type of relationship. For example, many Blacks in America, because of resentment over the persecution they have suffered, turned in the late 1960's toward the Black Power movement and became Muslims. Today, interracial congregations are a key to helping our Black brothers escape the deception of Islam.

Parent-Child Reconciliation

America has experienced a breakdown of basic parent-child relationships as well. Many men feel so inadequate in their roles as father and husband that they end up running away from their family responsibilities. Some men are abusive to their children. Others feel unable to communicate with them. Some do not know how to discipline. Others find the prospect of family fun and harmony to be out of their grasp.

And he will turn the hearts of the fathers to the children, and the hearts of the children to their fathers, lest I come and strike the earth with a curse.
                                                    Malachi 4:6

The Church is to be an extended family where reconciliation within nuclear families can be fostered. We share biblical principles of marriage and child rearing (including discipline) with one another; we can offer fellowship events in which parents and children can both take part.

One particular issue for family reconciliation is the challenging position of the single mother (or father). Family life is difficult enough as it is with two parents, so the obstacles confronting a single parent can seem overwhelming. Single parents, and children with only one parent, are the "widows and orphans" of our day.

> *...defend the fatherless, plead for the widow.*
> Isaiah 1:17

> *Pure and undefiled religion before God and the Father is this: to visit orphans and widows in their trouble....*
> James 1:27

Even though most single parent families are not actually widows and orphans, they face similar financial and emotional pressures. The congregational community can provide some sense of extended family and emotional support for them.

Women's Lib

Over the past quarter century a great deal of resentment has grown up among women against men in our

God's Answer to Alienation

country. By and large, this resentment is well founded. Women are fed up with sexual harassment on the job and with varying degrees of date rape in their social lives. It is out of that resentment that the women's lib movement has found so much momentum. Women are trying to establish a sense of independence and protection from the abuse of the male population.

The problem with the women's lib movement is that it offers no long-term solution for male-female relationships and does not deal with the source of their resentment. Men's abuse of women is demonic and carnal. But the hardening resentment and rebellion in women can result in an even worse demonic predicament. Thus, the Church must wage warfare against the Jezebel and witchcraft spirits in women. It must teach the principles of godly submission of women toward men. But that alone is insufficient if the Church does not offer a solution to the cause of men's abusing women.

Women throughout America feel abused because they are constantly besieged by a spirit of lust attacking them through men. Many of them have been abused physically. But almost all women have been abused in the spiritual sense by the intensity of the lust among men.

But I say to you that whoever looks at a women to lust for her has already committed adultery with her in his heart.
                                                              Matthew 5:28

Jesus taught that sexual sins done through the imagination are equivalent to ones that actually take place physically. Although not every woman in the country has been raped physically, many have had the experience of feeling as if she were being raped in the imaginations of men. Lust is not love, for love seeks to build up. Lust is, on the other hand, a perversion of love and wholesome sexuality. It defiles natural sexual desire with the added elements of obsessiveness and aggression. Lust seeks to inflict pain upon its victim.

A woman who has felt raped by the imagination of men's hearts experiences virtually the same kind of emotional pain, shame, and distress as one who was raped physically. By these standards, then, it would seem that almost every woman in America has been raped spiritually. This truth explains why many women reject the traditional female roles of wife and mother.

The Church is to provide a loving community where these hurts can be healed. Men should be challenged to repent of their lustful and violent attitudes. Women should find an environment where they can be treated with respect and purity. We should minister healing for the inner hurts women have experienced. Men must be encouraged to forgive women, and women to forgive men. A visitor should be able to witness the testimony of pure and reconciled relationships between men and women within the community.

The Isolation/Greed Syndrome

What makes so many people cooperate with the spirit of alienation in our society? The answer lies in the nature of greed and ambition.

God's Answer to Alienation

A man who isolates himself seeks his own desire....
Proverbs 18:1

When a man seeks to accomplish his own desire, he does not want to yield himself in submission and cooperation to relationships with other people. The world system inculcates values of materialism and pride, to the point people see themselves in competition with their neighbors. They need to beat out their coworkers for the next raise or promotion, or to "keep up with the Joneses" in purchasing a more expensive model of the latest product.

Family values are not emphasized as important in the workplace. The up-and-coming new employee is not encouraged to go home and spend time with his wife and children. The short-sighted goals of the company to produce immediate profits blind them to the fact that, in the long run, they would be better off with a career employee who has a stable family. The management will usually tell the aspiring young man that if he does not work many hours overtime and sacrifice his family life for the sake of the company, he will not be promoted. The rules of greed's game say that successful business and a balanced family life do not mix.

The same is true for the ministry. A minister primarily interested in the growth of his own ministry organization will not take time out to invest in personal relationships with others around him. Thus, alienation is pervasive in both the world and the Church because people are willing to isolate themselves in order to accomplish goals to bolster their egos. So until we are willing to give up selfish ambition and pride, we will never be able to break the pattern of isolation and alienation.

We need to be secure enough in who we are in the Lord that we do not have to become slaves to a scheme of getting ahead. It takes a secure person psychologically to know that building a relationship with another person has a higher value than competing against him. The Church must teach the biblical value that people are more important than things, and that relationships are more important than accomplishments.

Christianity Is Not a Religion

If Church life is to be an arena for interpersonal relationships and the ministry of reconciliation, we may have to alter some of our basic assumptions of what Christianity is. If Church life is to be the model of a spiritual community in the midst of an alienated society, we need to reevaluate structures and programs that we have taken for granted previously.

New Testament Christianity itself is not actually a religion. A *religion* is a system of rituals, holidays, rules of behavior, and moral laws that guide the lives of a group of people. God only designed one religion. That religion is not Christianity, but Judaism. Judaism is actually a religion. Christianity, on the other hand, is a faith relationship with God through Jesus the Messiah. Judaism is the religious context out of which faith in Jesus as the Messiah was birthed.

God's Answer to Alienation

Jesus did not come to start a new religion. He came to manifest the deeper heart relationship that was the ultimate goal of the Jewish religion. The purpose of the New Testament was not to come up with a new system of regulations to replace Judaism. Christianity is not a system of regulations; it is an ever-expanding network of personal relationships, starting with Jesus and His apostles, and extending to anyone who enters into relationship with them.

It is not my purpose to throw stones at organized religion, but to get us to rethink what our vision is of the Body of Christ.

That is, that God was in Christ reconciling the world to Himself...and has committed to us the word of reconciliation.
2 Corinthians 5:19

The Church is a body of people who extend the reconciliation ministry of Jesus to others, a model of heavenly community in the midst of an alienated world. The Church is a training center where those who have been reconciled to God learn to be reconciled to one another, and to bear witness of that reconciliation to a lost and dying world.

Chapter 4

The Five Streams

As a way to illustrate how the body of believers is to be unified in the endtimes, let me describe five major streams of the Church that represent the spectrum of what God is doing in the earth today. These five streams may be identified by the following labels: Holiness, Messianic, Covenant, Kingdom, and Faith.

These five are major movements within the Church, each with its own theological assumptions, terminology, perspective of looking at the Scriptures, revelations, and congregations that align themselves to the movement.

Different Streams of Revelation

The problem with these is many of the people in the movements have not been exposed—in a positive way—to the teachings and perspectives of the other streams.

They do not understand what God is saying through the other wings of the Church. If we are to become all that God wants us to be, we must be able to hear what God is saying to all the parts of the Church. Faith comes by hearing and hearing comes from understanding the revealed words of God (see Rom. 10:17). If we only hear what God is saying to one stream of the Church, then our faith will be strong only in the area of that stream of revelation. Thus each of these movements within the Church represents a stream of revelation from God.

Whatever movement of the Church we are alienated from is an area in which we do not grasp that stream of revelation. Whenever we reject a certain movement within the Church, we will be weak in the area of faith they represent.

For the equipping of the saints for the work of ministry, for the edifying of the body of Christ, till we all come to the unity of the faith and of the knowledge of the Son of God, to a perfect man, to the measure of the stature of the fullness of Christ.

Ephesians 4:12-13

God wants us to be complete in Him. We become complete in Him when we all come to the unity of the faith. Why? God embodies different streams of revelation in different streams of the Church. If we are to grasp the whole spectrum of the revelations of God, we must embrace the entire spectrum of the Church. As we embrace other streams of the Church, we learn to incorporate their revelation into our worldview. As we have

The Five Streams

more understanding, our faith grows; thus we become more complete.

As we grow in unity, we grow in understanding revelation from other parts of the Body of Christ. As we grow in unity, we grow in faith. Then, as our unity and our faith grows, we become complete in Him.

Do not discard other streams of the Church that you may be unfamiliar with. If you do, you will miss the revelation God has given them and be incomplete in your own faith. You will not only be incomplete in your personal faith, but also the Body of Christ as a whole will not reach its maturity where "all come to the unity of the faith." Our faith, our unity, and our calling are all tied together.

Let us look briefly at each of these streams of the Church.

Holiness

The Holiness movement emphasizes such themes as repentance, purity, revival, zeal, the wrath of God, the fear of God, humility, and the sobering aspects of the truths of the Scriptures. Ministers within the Holiness movement tend to be well read in classic Christian devotional literature and revivalist writings. Their worship services include a time of quietness for listening to God and for cleansing one's heart of carnal desires. Their hard-hitting messages at times drive people to weep in response to the lost condition of the world.

They believe strongly in separating themselves from worldly or carnal activities, inculcating in their members a hatred for the things of this world (see 1 Jn. 2:15). They are willing to minister in situations that require self-sacrifice, suffering, and self-denial. Their goal is to re-establish the awe and reverence of God's sovereign authority that was devalued by a humanistic view of the Scriptures. People in this movement see God as a consuming fire and are jealous for His honor and justice.

Messianic

The Messianic movement is concerned with restoring the Jewish roots of the Christian faith. Here people believe that the Church moved away from some of God's original purposes when it became Gentilized in the third and fourth centuries, adopting certain pagan practices and philosophies into the format of the Church.

The Messianic movement points out that Scriptures mandate a priority in evangelism to the Jew, and that a revival among the Jewish people is a significant prerequisite for the Second Coming of the Messiah. They maintain that New Covenant Scriptures cannot be interpreted in any way that contradicts canonized revelation already given in the Law and the Prophets. They see a continuing validity in the symbolic and prophetic meaning of the biblical feasts of Israel.

They view the regathering of the Jews to the nation of Israel today as the initial stages of the fulfillment of the prophecies of Isaiah, Jeremiah, and Ezekiel. In their view, the restoration of the nation of Israel is a foundational element in God's plan to establish the Kingdom of God upon the earth.

Covenant

The Covenant movement emphasizes such topics as relationships in the Body of Christ, character building, integrity, commitment, responsibility, and a right order for congregational government. Their members are dedicated and loyal and tend to be involved in a wide variety of projects to make the gospel relevant to practical social needs. They are strong in defending family values, and lead the legal battle for religious freedom in America.

People in the Covenant movement have a positive understanding of discipleship and of the proper role for submitting to authority in the family, church, and government. They emphasize home cell group reproduction and seek to develop many of their members for positions of lay leadership. Having a love for justice, they are concerned with establishing a biblical judicial process within the Church. They have a well-developed concept of the roles of deacons, elders, and the fivefold gift ministries.

They are a faithful people and are committed to building networks of relationships throughout the Body of Christ. They also believe in teamwork ministry.

Kingdom

The Kingdom movement sees not only the spiritual authority of the individual believer, but also the widespread dominion that God has granted to the Church as a whole. They have a strong view of the Church as a present demonstration of the coming kingdom. They see the Church as the embodiment and representative of the Kingdom of God during this transitional age. Although the Church is not the final stage of the Kingdom, it has been given the Spirit of the Kingdom.

These people have a strong understanding of how the Church community can impact a nation, including its government, social structure, educational system, and economy. They appreciate the positive role that the Church as an institution has played in the course of history. They also have an ongoing vision of how the gospel can bring whole nations and societies under the lordship of Jesus.

In their eyes, the Church is a spiritual form of government that will eventually exercise rulership over all the systems of government of this present world. People in the Kingdom movement believe in redeeming every vehicle of media and culture for the sake of the gospel, including television, dance, drama, and art. They have also made headway in dealing with major social problems such as racism, crime, housing, and governmental reform.

Faith

The Faith movement emphasizes the positive benefits of the gospel for every individual believer. They deal with such topics as the present righteousness of the believer, spiritual authority over demons, healing, prosperity, the power of the tongue, and victorious living. They also emphasize the distinction between soul and spirit, and that each believer should see himself as a new spiritual creation in the eyes of God.

People in the Faith movement have a strong respect for letting the individual hear from God and act according to his own conscience. Rejecting dead religious ritualism and phony theological sophistication, they encourage their members to base their speech, thoughts, and actions on the Word of God. Their meetings are dynamic, uplifting, and fun.

They believe that miracles occur when spiritual principles in the Bible are correctly understood and applied. They view faith as an actual, indwelling force that enters a believer as he meditates on the Word of God. That faith then has the potential to produce creative results through the active cooperation of the believer himself.

Perspectives on the Gospel

In order to illustrate the different perspectives of these movements, let us review briefly how they might deal with such topics as the Great Commission, the birth of the Church at Pentecost, prophecy, and finances.

The Holiness movement would point out that the Great Commission centers on calling people to repent.

And that repentance and remission of sins should be preached in His name to all nations....
Luke 24:47

Now when they heard this, they were cut to the heart, and said to Peter and the rest of the apostles, "Men and brethren, what shall we do?" Then Peter said to them, "Repent...."

Acts 2:37-38

Then he said to the multitudes that came out to be baptized by him, "Brood of vipers! Who warned you to flee from the wrath to come?"

Luke 3:7

The Messianic movement would point out the priority of Jewish evangelism.

For I am not ashamed of the gospel of Christ, for it is the power of God to salvation for everyone who believes, for the Jew first and also for the Greek.

Romans 1:16

For I could wish that I myself were accursed from Christ for my brethren, my countrymen according to the flesh, who are Israelites....

Romans 9:3-4

...and you shall be witnesses to Me in Jerusalem, and in all Judea and Samaria, and to the end of the earth.

Acts 1:8

The Covenant movement would notice the discipleship and relational aspects of the gospel.

Go therefore and make disciples of all the nations... teaching them to observe all things that I have commanded you....

Matthew 28:19-20

...for he who does not love his brother whom he has seen, how can he love God whom he has not seen?
1 John 4:20

..."This cup is the new covenant in My blood, which is shed for you."
Luke 22:20

The Kingdom movement would show that the gospel is challenging the nations with a new world order.

Go therefore and make disciples of all the nations....
Matthew 28:19

And this gospel of the kingdom will be preached in all the world as a witness to all the nations....
Matthew 24:14

..."The kingdoms of this world have become the kingdoms of our Lord and of His Christ, and He shall reign forever and ever."
Revelation 11:15

The Faith movement would emphasize the power of the Holy Spirit as well as faith to accompany the gospel with healing, deliverance, and miracles.

"And these signs will follow those who believe: In My name they will cast out demons...they will lay hands on the sick and they will recover." ... And they went out and preached everywhere, the Lord working with them

and confirming the word through the accompanying signs. Amen.

Mark 16:17-18,20

They also would emphasize that the key element of salvation is not so much repentance, but believing in what Jesus has already done for us on the cross.

Perspectives on the Early Church

How would these different movements look at the birth of the Church? The Holiness movement would point out the place of repentance, the fear of God, and sacrificial living.

And with many other words he testified and exhorted them, saying, "Be saved from this perverse generation." ... *Then fear came upon every soul.... Now all who believed were together...and sold their possessions and goods, and divided them among all, as anyone had need.*

Acts 2:40,43-45

The Messianic movement would point out that the revival took place on the Jewish holy day of Shavuot (Pentecost), that all the original believers were orthodox Jews, and that the Church was a fulfillment of Old Testament prophecies.

When the Day of Pentecost [Shavuot] had fully come.... And there were dwelling in Jerusalem Jews, devout men, from every nation under heaven.

Acts 2:1,5

...Men of Judea and all who dwell in Jerusalem, let this be known to you.... But this is what was spoken by the prophet Joel.

Acts 2:14,16

Now Peter and John went up together to the temple at the hour of prayer....

Acts 3:1

The Covenant movement would point out the unity and fellowship among the believers.

When the Day of Pentecost had fully come, they were all with one accord in one place.

Acts 2:1

And they continued steadfastly in the apostles' doctrine and fellowship, in the breaking of bread, and in prayers. ... Now all who believed were together, and had all things in common, and sold their possessions and goods, and divided them among all, as anyone had need. So continuing daily with one accord in the temple, and breaking bread from house to house....

Acts 2:42,44-46

The Kingdom movement would show how the early Church turned the world upside down and brought the gospel before kings and potentates.

But when they did not find them, they dragged Jason and some brethren to the rulers of the city, crying out,

"These who have turned the world upside down have come here too."
Acts 17:6

"I think myself happy, King Agrippa, because today I shall answer for myself before you...."
Acts 26:2

"For the king, before whom I also speak freely, knows these things; for I am convinced that none of these things escapes his attention, since this thing was not done in a corner." ... *Then Agrippa said to Festus, "This man might have been set free if he had not appealed to Caesar."*
Acts 26:26,32

The Faith movement would point to the miraculous healing power of faith in the name of Jesus.

And fixing his eyes on him, with John, Peter said, "Look at us." ... *Then Peter said, "...In the name of Jesus Christ of Nazareth, rise up and walk." And he took him by the right hand and lifted him up, and immediately his feet and ankle bones received strength.*
Acts 3:4,6-7

And His name, through faith in His name, has made this man strong, whom you see and know. Yes, the faith which comes through Him has given him the perfect soundness in the presence of you all.
Acts 3:16

The early Church was concerned with both purity and power. They related intimately with one another, had a deep awareness of their Jewish heritage, and saw themselves as the rightful heirs of Kingdom government.

Perspectives on Prophecy

How would these different movements look at the role and function of prophecy? The Holiness movement would cite extensive passages in the Prophets that deal with the coming judgment of God upon the world. They would see prophecy as primarily to warn people of the wrath to come.

> *For thus says the Lord God of Israel to me: "Take this wine cup of fury from My hand, and cause all the nations, to whom I send you, to drink it. And they will drink and stagger and go mad because of the sword that I will send among them."*
> Jeremiah 25:15-16

> *So the angel thrust his sickle into the earth and gathered the vine of the earth, and threw it into the great winepress of the wrath of God. And the winepress was trampled outside the city, and blood came out of the winepress....*
> Revelation 14:19-20

The Messianic movement would point to the sweep of prophecies that deal with the restoration of the nation of Israel and the calling of the Jewish people.

For Zion's sake I will not hold My peace, and for Jerusalem's sake I will not rest, until her righteousness goes forth as brightness, and her salvation as a lamp that burns.

Isaiah 62:1

So Zerubbabel...and Jeshua...rose up and began to build the house of God which is in Jerusalem; and the prophets of God were with them, helping them.

Ezra 5:2

And I heard the number of those who were sealed. One hundred and forty-four thousand of all the tribes of the children of Israel were sealed.

Revelation 7:4

The Covenant movement deals with prophecy as part of body-life ministry, in which believers in a local congregation edify and exhort one another. They also see prophecy as part of the fivefold ministry gifts that equip the saints.

But he who prophesies speaks edification and exhortation and comfort to men. He who speaks in a tongue edifies himself, but he who prophesies edifies the church.

1 Corinthians 14:3-4

And He Himself gave some to be apostles, some prophets, some evangelists, and some pastors and teachers, for the equipping of the saints for the work of ministry, for the edifying of the body of Christ.

Ephesians 4:11-12

The Kingdom movement would see prophecy addressing nations, challenging governments, and changing the course of history.

See, I have this day set you over the nations and over the kingdoms....
Jeremiah 1:10

And He changes the times and the seasons; He removes kings and raises up kings....
Daniel 2:21

And he said to me, "You must prophesy again about many peoples, nations, tongues, and kings."
Revelation 10:11

The Faith movement sees prophecy as speaking forth the word of God with creative power. Speaking the *rhema* word of God by faith causes God's will to come to pass in our lives.

...in the presence of Him whom he believed—God, who gives life to the dead and calls those things which do not exist as though they did.
Romans 4:17

For assuredly, I say to you, whoever...does not doubt in his heart, but believes that those things he says will be done, he will have whatever he says.
Mark 11:23

All five movements see themselves as exercising prophecy in the way intended in the Bible. In fact, all five movements are prophetic in nature and are restoring some aspect of prophetic ministry.

Perspectives on Finances

Finally, let us look at how these five movements deal with finances. The Holiness movement would emphasize the sinfulness of greed and the need to be free from every attachment to material things.

> *For we brought nothing into this world, and it is certain we can carry nothing out. ... But those who desire to be rich fall into temptation and a snare, and into many foolish and harmful lusts which drown men in destruction and perdition. For the love of money is a root of all kinds of evil, for which some have strayed from the faith in their greediness, and pierced themselves through with many sorrows.*
> 1 Timothy 6:7,9-10

The Messianic movement would show that the promises of prosperity come from God's covenant with Abraham, that God placed the gold and silver in the world for the building of His temple, and that the wealth of the nations is destined to stream toward Israel's prosperity.

> *...The wealth of the Gentiles shall come to you. ... Surely the coastlands shall wait for Me; and the ships of*

The Five Streams

Tarshish will come first, to bring your sons from afar, their silver and gold with them…that men may bring to you the wealth of the Gentiles….

Isaiah 60:5,9-11

And whoever is left in any place where he dwells, let the men of his place help him with silver and gold, with goods and livestock, besides the freewill offerings for the house of God which is in Jerusalem.

Ezra 1:4

The Covenant movement would emphasize principles of integrity, responsibility, and character in dealing with one's work, financial commitments, and giving. We are stewards of God's resources.

Nor did we eat anyone's bread free of charge, but worked with labor and toil night and day, that we might not be a burden to any of you.

2 Thessalonians 3:8

…If anyone will not work, neither shall he eat.

2 Thessalonians 3:10

…"Lord, you delivered to me five talents; look, I have gained five more talents besides them." His lord said to him, "Well done, good and faithful servant; you were faithful over a few things, I will make you ruler over many things…."

Matthew 25:20-21

The Kingdom movement would point out that throughout history, nations that turned to the gospel have prospered. The righteous foundations of the Church affect the overall economic climate of a country. After all, all of the natural resources in the earth belong to God.

> *"The silver is Mine, and the gold is Mine," says the Lord of hosts.*
>
> Haggai 2:8

> *So he called ten of his servants, delivered to them ten minas, and said to them, "Do business till I come."*
>
> Luke 19:13

> *So King Solomon surpassed all the kings of the earth in riches and wisdom.*
>
> 1 Kings 10:23

The Faith movement teaches that it is God's will to prosper us. They would note that giving leads to receiving; thus faith prosperity is based on faith generosity. Prosperity is a positive blessing of God's covenant. Our prosperity then bears witness to God's goodness and to His ability to provide for us.

> *Beloved, I pray that you may prosper in all things and be in health, just as your soul prospers.*
>
> 3 John 2

The Five Streams

Give, and it will be given to you: good measure, pressed down, shaken together, and running over will be put into your bosom....

Luke 6:38

Just to show how different perspectives can be gleaned from a single verse, an eye for holiness would see God's warning against greed in First Timothy 6:17: "Command those who are rich in this present age not to be haughty, nor to trust in uncertain riches..." while an eye for faith would see God's grace to bless us with prosperity: "...but in the living God, who gives us richly all things to enjoy."

All of these perspectives are true, each representing different facets of the same jewel. It reminds one of the story of the six blind men who tried to describe what an elephant was, except each one had felt a different part of the elephant: its tusk, its ear, its tail, its trunk, its side, and its leg.

Pride Brings Deception

We are all sure of what we know. We know what God has revealed to us. The problem, however, is not in what we know, but in what we do not know. The nature of ignorance says that not only is there more truth that we do not know, but also that we are unaware of the fact we do not know it.

All of us have areas of spiritual blindness. That means that all of us are deceived to some degree or another. We

The Five Streams

are not deceived in our general faith about Jesus, salvation, and the Bible, but we each have pockets of deception in unsanctified areas of our lives.

> *If we say that we have no sin* [spiritual blindness], *we deceive ourselves….*
>
> 1 John 1:8

If we try to insist that we are not deceived in any way, or that we cannot ever be deceived, we make it impossible for us to break out of the deception we are already in. Stubbornness only makes deception worse.

The best way out of deception is to admit that we all have areas of deception. If I admit that I can be deceived, then I am open to learn and to be corrected out of those deceptions. Part of spiritual warfare is to tear down vain imaginations and false illusions (see 2 Cor. 10:5). The key to freedom from deception is to maintain a teachable heart. Let us always be willing to learn.

> *Then some of the Pharisees…said to Him, "Are we blind also?" Jesus said to them, "If you were blind, you would have no sin; but now you say, 'We see.' Therefore your sin remains."*
>
> John 9:40-41

Every sin carries with it its own blindness. Whenever we sin, we are blind. All deception comes from pride. All pride causes deception. The very thing you are most proud of may be where you are deceived.

Humility is the only way out of deception; it is the only safeguard against it. If we ask God to show us our unknown sins, He will do so (see Ps. 51:6). Deception is false faith. Humility tears down false faith, just as the Word of God builds up true faith. Humility is an essential aspect of spiritual warfare.

Truth Is Alive

The biblical concept of truth is not a set of facts or a philosophical system—truth is alive. In fact, truth is a person.

> *Jesus said to him, "I am the way, the truth, and the life...."*
>
> John 14:6

The Western secular mind looks for truth as it does data or information. The biblical worldview sees truth as an expression of the personality of God. When Jesus stood in front of Pilate, Pilate asked Him what truth was. Jesus could not answer him with a statement of a fact because He Himself was the embodiment of truth.

> *Pilate said to Him, "What is truth?"...*
>
> John 18:38

It was as if Pilate had said, "Jesus, show me a picture of the Messiah." There was nothing Jesus could do but stand there.

Living truth is an expression of God's character and personality. *True* means "true-blue," trustworthy, having integrity. A *personality* is a dynamic thing. It has inward momentum and a creative tension. Truth, therefore, when it is alive, always has an aspect of dynamic tension. Real truth cannot be stated without this dynamic tension. Thus, truth is factual, but it is not a fact.

For example, what is the nature of Jesus' divinity? Is He man or is He God? To only say that He is man or that He is God would not fully represent the situation. His divinity and His humanity exist in a living dynamic tension.

Similarly, I am a father to my children. Could I say that my fatherhood is affectionate or authoritative? It is impossible to divorce the two contrasting elements. The very word *father* speaks of both authority and affection. One without the other would not communicate the living truth.

God created both male and female in His own image. When male and female come together in marriage, there is living creative power that can give birth to a child.

So it is in chemistry as well. The positive and negative valences of electrons and protons exist in a dynamic tension that holds matter together.

Dynamic Tension of Truth

Scriptural truth contains this dynamic tension. To say that God does not want you to be greedy and that God wants to prosper you are contrasting sides of the same truth. In another example, Jesus was of the lineage of

David according to the flesh and was the Son of God according to the Spirit (see Rom. 1:3-4). Also, God's wrath will be poured out on the earth by the same act of the Spirit that will bring glory and comfort to His saints.

> *Most assuredly, I say to you, unless a grain of wheat falls into the ground and dies, it remains alone; but if it dies, it produces much grain. He who loves his life will lose it, and he who hates his life in this world will keep it for eternal life.*
> John 12:24-25

> *I have been crucified with Christ; it is no longer I who live, but Christ lives in me....*
> Galatians 2:20

> *Blessed are those who mourn, for they shall be comforted.*
> Matthew 5:4

This dynamic nature of truth guarantees that a merely intellectual or philosophical investigation is not capable of discovering it. The personality aspect of truth is embraced by the heart or spirit of man, not calculated by mental analysis.

> *..."I thank You, Father, Lord of heaven and earth, that You have hidden these things from the wise and prudent and have revealed them to babes."*
> Matthew 11:25

When we cling to only one aspect of the truth, it eventually becomes death to us. In whatever movement or stream of revelation in the Church we find ourselves, we must not get stuck in a one-dimensional view of the truth. People in one stream of the Church often interpret the revelation coming from a different stream in a negative light. We tend to think that other people are unbalanced.

The problem is not so much what the other person is saying, but what he is leaving unsaid. There is certainly nothing wrong with preaching it is God's will for us to prosper, but if we never mention that we need to purge ourselves of greed and ambition, we are bound to end up with carnal desires. Likewise, neither is there anything wrong with telling someone that he should not be greedy, but if we do not preach God's blessings and prosperity, people will not be able to enter into God's provision.

It is true that the Kingdom movement has had a great revelation of God's glorious calling and destiny for the Church. But if there is no mention of the continuing validity of the biblical promises to Israel, people will miss the revelation that the restoration of Israel is also a manifestation of the same Kingdom purposes of God.

Faith and Faithfulness

The Hebrew word *emunah* can be translated as either "faith" or "faithfulness." In the biblical view, faith and faithfulness cannot be separated.

> *...Nevertheless, when the Son of Man comes, will He really find faith on the earth?*
>
> Luke 18:8

When Jesus comes back, He will be looking for people who are both faithful and faith-filled. Lack of faithfulness will cause faith to crumble. Trying to be faithful without faith is impossible; covenant integrity and word-of-faith power go hand in hand.

> *Therefore I say to you, whatever things you ask when you pray, believe that you receive them, and you will have them. And whenever you stand praying, if you have anything against anyone, forgive him, that your Father in heaven may also forgive you your trespasses.*
>
> Mark 11:24-25

Our faith has the power to move mountains. But if we are not faithful to forgive those around us, our mountain-moving faith will not work.

The Two-Edged Sword

It is possible to demonstrate the contrasting dynamic tension of nearly every truth in Scripture. Biblical revelation, in other words, is a two-edged sword.

> *For the word of God is living and powerful, and sharper than any two-edged sword, piercing even to the division*

The Five Streams

of soul and spirit, and of joints and marrow, and is a discerner of the thoughts and intents of the heart.
Hebrews 4:12

When a soldier holds a two-edged sword in his hand, one edge points at the enemy and the other edge points back toward himself. The Word of God is described as a sword for spiritual warfare against the enemy (see Eph. 6:17). In Hebrews 4:6 it is also described as a surgeon's scalpel that cuts into the innermost motivations and intentions of our heart. Thus the Word of God is a weapon of warfare for us to take vengeance upon the world, as well as a weapon of discipline in which we attack and purge the lusts of our own heart.

...bringing every thought into captivity to the obedience of Christ, and being ready to punish all disobedience when your obedience is fulfilled.
2 Corinthians 10:5-6

When we preach the Word, we have to wield it in such a way that both edges of the sword are used. The blade must cut in both directions. Our enemy is both sin and Satan. At times the key element is to resist Satan; at other times it is to repent of sin. Heaven and hell are both real. To preach the fires of hell without the glories of heaven is condemnation. To preach the glories of Heaven without warning people of the fires of hell is to lull them into a false security.

Furthermore, we are saved by faith without any works of our own effort. But it is also true that faith without

The Five Streams

corresponding actions is dead. We need to take upon ourselves the yoke of obedience to Jesus, but also know that His yoke is easy and light. We need to crucify the flesh daily so that we are not yielding to selfish desires, but also know that if we delight ourselves in God, He will give us the desires of our heart. (See Ephesians 2:8-9 and James 2:26; Matthew 11:29-30; Luke 9:23 and Psalm 37:4.)

We must digest the revelation that comes from all five of these streams if we are to be complete and mature in Jesus. We receive the parts of the teaching that are correct and expel the parts that are wrong.

Test all things; hold fast to what is good.
1 Thessalonians 5:21

We are not in the Church to push our agenda of a particular doctrine or a particular stream of revelation. Each one of us has to incorporate in our own hearts this spectrum of God's revelation so our lives can reflect the multifaceted personality of Jesus. Our congregations should incorporate the various elements of these streams of the Church so we, as a body, can also reflect the full personality of Jesus.

Chapter 5

Simply Jesus

If the Church is to be what God has called us to be, then Jesus must be restored to His place as the focus of all our ministries. Jesus is to be recognized and worshiped as the Head of the Church. Our laying hold of Jesus' identity as Head of the Church brings us into our role as the Body of Christ. Thus the more we understand His role as the Head, the more we will understand our role as a body.

And He is the head of the body, the church, who is the beginning, the firstborn from the dead, that in all things He may have the preeminence.
Colossians 1:18

If Jesus is the Head of the Body, then He is the leader and director. If He is the Head of the Church, then we should do what He tells us to do. Our activities should be His program, not ours. If we recognize His ownership of the Church, ministers will not have to struggle with feelings of possessiveness and competition. Also, congregational life will be freer and more enjoyable as we relinquish ownership back to Him.

Jesus Is Preeminent

If Jesus is the Head of the Church, then He is to have preeminence in everything we do. The Church is God's vehicle of leadership within the earth (replacing the old order of Adam's fall and Satan's rebellion). Jesus' role as Head of the Church means that ultimately He is to be the Head of everything that happens on the planet. Before His leadership can be fully established throughout the globe, though, it must first be established within the Church. How can He exercise His lordship over the entire earth if the Church is not submitted to Him?

The Church community is to be the arena in which Jesus' leadership is clearly demonstrated. People should be able to take note by who we are and how we act that Jesus is the one in charge.

If we are to be what God has called us to be as the Church, then our first job is to make Him preeminent. Everything we do should give Him glory, make Him famous, and reflect positively on His honor. Our actions and attitudes should demonstrate that the Kingdom, the power, and the glory belong to Him (see Mt. 6:13). He should get the credit for the good things that happen in our midst. His reputation should be enhanced, not maligned, by what we do.

If Jesus is preeminent, then He is our top priority. He should take first place in everything we do—the focal point of our worship, preaching, and fellowship. Even the role of the Holy Spirit is to testify about Jesus and to glorify Him (Jn. 15:26; 16:14). We as the Church are the dwelling place and vehicle of the Holy Spirit in the earth. Our job, as the instrument of the Holy Spirit, is to point people toward Jesus. Our programs and activities should be evaluated as to what degree they give attention to Jesus. The more we lift up Jesus, the more people will be drawn to the Kingdom of God (see Jn. 12:32).

Biblical Knowledge, or Knowing Jesus

Our doctrines and teachings are not to demonstrate how great our understanding of the Scriptures are, but to enhance people's relationship with Jesus. We are not so much interested in someone's teaching (be it Holiness, Messianic, Covenant, Kingdom, or Faith), as we are in being a good example of the life and love of Jesus.

> *And though I have the gift of prophecy, and understand all mysteries and all knowledge, and though I have all faith, so that I could remove mountains, but have not love, I am nothing.*
>
> 1 Corinthians 13:2

God is not impressed with the depth of our understanding of His mysteries. He wants us to love one another and to be like Jesus. So if Jesus is to be preeminent in all things, we must return to the simplicity of loving Him. The emphasis in our teaching is not on what we know, but on Jesus. Sometimes we spend so much time searching the Scriptures to reinforce our doctrinal positions that we miss the obvious simplicity of a personal relationship with Him.

You search the Scriptures, for in them you think you have eternal life; and these are they which testify of Me.
John 5:39

It seems amazing to us that the Pharisees and the experts in the Law could have had so much knowledge of the Scripture and missed Jesus. They studied the Bible, but missed out on the relationship with the very person the Bible speaks about. This can happen not only to an orthodox rabbi or to an unsaved theology professor, but even to the most dedicated and sincere believer. In the case of the unsaved, they miss knowing the Lord in the first place. In the case of the believer, the danger is of drifting away from the vibrant and enjoyable quality of our relationship with God.

For the rabbi or the theologian, it is an issue of salvation; in a believer's case, it is an issue of emphasis. Emphasis is not to be on our movements, ministries, worship styles, or agendas, but on Jesus. It is not to be on the prophetic callings and revelations that God has given us, but on Him. Even when we are correct in what we say, we can be wrong if our focus has shifted away from

Jesus. Emphasis on our own rightness can ruin the freshness of our relationship with Jesus.

Ministry vs. First Love

Jesus must be more important to us than our ministry. God tested Abraham to see if he would give up his son Isaac. Not only did Abraham love Isaac, but all of Abraham's hopes and dreams for the future were bound up in him. Isaac embodied the sum total of Abraham's mission and prophetic calling. Abraham could lose not only his beloved son, but everything he had invested a lifetime of faith and struggle to produce. Abraham's entire purpose in life was wrapped up in Isaac.

God's ultimate test is to ask you to let go of the very things He has called you to do. God gives every person a mission in life. But even that mission is not as important to God as your personal relationship with Him. In the Church, though, we can get so caught up with our mission in life that we ruin our first love.

And you have persevered and have patience, and have labored for My name's sake and have not become weary. Nevertheless I have this against you, that you have left your first love.

Revelation 2:3-4

God wants to have first place in our lives. A dedicated believer does not have too much trouble giving up the sinful things of the world and the flesh. But are we willing to let go of the things God has called us to do in order to keep God first place in our life? Are we so attached to the prophetic purposes of God that we are ruining our childlike joy of knowing Him?

Satan tempted Christ in the wilderness concerning the very mission that He had come to accomplish. Jesus came into this world to redeem all kingdoms and authorities. Satan tried to offer Him those kingdoms by appealing to a psychological need in Jesus to accomplish that mission. Obviously Jesus was not going to sin in the carnal sense of the word. Satan's only hope at temptation was to press Him to put His ministry ahead of His personal devotion to the Father. Have we failed the same test?

And though I bestow all my goods to feed the poor, and though I give my body to be burned, but have not love, it profits me nothing.
                                                1 Corinthians 13:3

God is not so much interested in how much we can accomplish for the Kingdom of God as He is in the quality of our love. If we become psychologically attached to the things God has called us to do, then we may be unknowingly caught up in serving ourselves more than in serving God. If our sense of mission becomes narrow-minded, we run the subtle danger of becoming like a Pharisee. Religious hypocrisy awaits us if we do not return to the simplicity of knowing Jesus.

Revelation vs. Love

We demonstrate real maturity when we let go of our ministry agendas and prophetic revelations to return to the joy of our first love.

Love never fails. But whether there are prophecies, they will fail; whether there are tongues, they will cease; whether there is knowledge, it will vanish away.
1 Corinthians 13:8

We should not get hung up on the things we think we know, because we really only know part of the truth.

For we know in part and we prophesy in part.
1 Corinthians 13:9

Pushing other people to recognize our part of the picture is childish behavior. When we think our ministry and calling are more important than what God is doing in the Body of Christ in general, we are still immature. To be mature is to return to the simplicity of loving Jesus and so loving our brother.

When I was a child, I spoke as a child, I understood as a child, I thought as a child; but when I became a man, I put away childish things.
1 Corinthians 13:11

Lack of appreciation for what God is doing through others also indicates immaturity. It is childish to be compulsive and myopic about what you are called to do. Real maturity is to come back to a place of childlike freedom and love.

> *Now I say that the heir, as long as he is a child, does not differ at all from a slave, though he is master of all, but is under guardians and stewards until the time appointed by the father.*
>
> Galatians 4:1-2

The process of maturity in Christ has three general stages: first there is a childish and simple joy of knowing Jesus; second is the process of discipleship in which we learn the various aspects of the Kingdom of God; and finally, there is a return to that first childlike simplicity of knowing Jesus.

The Process of Discipleship

There is no way of avoiding this process of maturing. When we first come to the Lord, our lives are in a mess, spiritually. We do not even realize how messed up we are. Without any more responsibility than a nursing baby in diapers, we enter into a relationship with our heavenly Father by grace. There is so much that we are ignorant of and so many areas of our lives that need to be fixed up. God then puts us through an extended program of education and restoration. Because God loves us, He wants to repair what is broken in our lives.

Each time we learn a new aspect of the Kingdom of God, we become totally consumed with that revelation.

We burn with desire to share with someone else the thing that has so greatly helped us. However, we must watch that we do not get stuck in any one particular stage of revelation. There is always more to learn. We must keep going and not think that we have "arrived." God always has something else to share with us, and He often does so through other people. We need to hear what God is saying to us through another person, even if that person is imperfect in many areas of his life.

It is inevitable that we must go through a period of training. We need to learn all the areas of revelation represented by the various streams and movements within the Church. After all, before we were born again into the Kingdom of God, we did not know anything about the Kingdom. As we start the salvation process, almost every area of our life needs to be straightened out.

As we stay with this process of discipleship and restoration, we reemerge with the childlike simplicity in which we began.

> *Even so we, when we were children, were in bondage under the elements of the world. But when the fullness of the time had come, God sent forth His Son, born of a woman, born under the law, to redeem those who were under the law, that we might receive the adoption as sons. And because you are sons, God has sent forth the Spirit of His Son into your hearts, crying out, "Abba, Father!"*
>
> Galatians 4:3-6

We start out as a child, as a baby. Then we go through a process of tutelage and maturation. The goal of our maturity is the wholesome place of sonship where we enjoy a loving relationship with our heavenly Father. Thus we return to a childlike simplicity in a renewed way. That is the fruit of maturity.

What Do We Preach?

We also return to the simplicity of Jesus in the way we preach. Now, the world is made complicated by sin. Satan is the author of confusion, but God's solutions are simple. Our perversions and rebellion against God have made the problems so complicated that we find it difficult to see the simplicity of the solutions. We must watch out that we do not get caught up in the complications of the world's problems. We need to stay with the simplicity of Jesus' solution.

> *But I fear, lest somehow, as the serpent deceived Eve by his craftiness, so your minds may be corrupted from the simplicity that is in Christ. For if he who comes preaches another Jesus whom we have not preached…you may well put up with it!*
>
> 2 Corinthians 11:3-4

If our preaching is to have the power of God, then we must return to the simplicity of preaching Jesus. The early disciples preached a powerful gospel that had miraculous results. Yet there was still much of the Kingdom of God and of biblical interpretation they did not know. What did they do? They preached Jesus, baptized people in the Holy Spirit, and healed the sick.

If we this day are judged for a good deed done to a helpless man, by what means he has been made well, let it be known to you all, and to all the people of Israel, that by the name of Jesus Christ of Nazareth, whom you crucified, whom God raised from the dead, by Him this man stands here before you whole.

Acts 4:9-10

The simplicity of their message did not detract from the power. The people around them saw that the power was coming from Jesus. It was obviously not the apostles' theological sophistication that caused the man to be healed—it had to be Jesus.

Now when they saw the boldness of Peter and John, and perceived that they were uneducated and untrained men, they marveled. And they realized that they had been with Jesus.

Acts 4:13

Many of us find this hard to grasp because we have been affected by intellectual pride. Spiritual and intellectual pride go back to the root of the sinful nature of man. It was the fruit of the tree of knowledge that first turned us away from God.

Inherent in the message of the gospel is its simplicity. By its very nature, the gospel frustrates religious pride and hypocrisy. Part of the power of the message of the cross comes from its annihilation of human wisdom.

For the message of the cross is foolishness to those who are perishing, but to us who are being saved it is the

> *power of God. For it is written: "I will destroy the wisdom of the wise...." Where is the wise?... For since, in the wisdom of God, the world through wisdom did not know God, it pleased God through the foolishness of the message preached to save those who believe.*
>
> 1 Corinthians 1:18-21

We all need to fight our way out of the trap of wanting people to respect us for our wisdom. The world tries to make us submit to its false standard of rationality and humanism, but the world's wisdom does not serve us. We do not owe anything to the flesh (see Rom. 8:12). We do not have to ask the world for its approval of our faith.

Preaching Jesus

Jesus is our message. The world needs Jesus. Although they do not want to admit they need Jesus, there is no other solution to the state of death and damnation they are in. The world is sinking in its sin toward hell under the wrath of God. Now is not a time for human rationality. A desperate situation requires a radical solution—Jesus is the answer. We need to fight to make sure the question does not get diverted to some other issue.

> *Then Philip went down to the city of Samaria and preached Christ to them. ... Then Philip opened his mouth, and beginning at this Scripture, preached Jesus to him.*
>
> Acts 8:5,35

To them God willed to make known what are the riches of the glory of this mystery among the Gentiles: which is Christ in you, the hope of glory. Him we preach....
                                            Colossians 1:27-28

Jesus must be restored as the primary topic of our sermons. He is the priority of our preaching. We want to preach all the truths of the Holiness, Messianic, Covenant, Kingdom, and Faith movements, but our emphasis must remain on the person of Jesus. If any of those other truths gain a priority over the message of Jesus Himself, we defeat our own purpose. Christ is to be preeminent in all things, including our teaching and preaching. The truths of the Scriptures are to be preached according to how they relate to the person of Jesus and with the emphasis always on Him.

All Wisdom and Knowledge in Jesus

All spiritual truths come out of the person of Jesus. It is not what we know, but whom we know. Through Jesus we come to know God.

Jesus said to him, "Have I been with you so long, and yet you have not known Me, Philip? He who has seen Me has seen the Father; so how can you say, 'Show us the Father'?"

John 14:9

...attaining to all riches of the full assurance of understanding, to the knowledge of the mystery of God, both of

the Father and of Christ, in whom are hidden all the treasures of wisdom and knowledge.

Colossians 2:2-3

There is no revelation of God that is separate from Jesus. We do not learn a new truth, but rather discover new and sparkling aspects of the personality of Jesus.

The world throws counterfeits and temptations at us in order to make us feel that we are missing something. If we do not buy this product, we will miss some exciting experience. If a teenager does not try this drug, if a man does not commit this adultery, if we do not learn about this new discovery, if we are not current with what is happening in the news—we will have missed out on something essential.

Let us remember this right from the beginning: The world has nothing to offer. There is not anything that is good for me that cannot be found in the person of Jesus. I never have to succumb to the world's temptation that says I might miss out on some great experience.

The life of Jesus continues to expand and grow in us every day. His personality within us is new and alive every morning. Anything we could ever need or want in life can be found in our relationship with Jesus. He is the resource and fountain of every good thing. When we have Jesus, we do not need anything else.

Headship Demands Unity

Jesus is the Head of the Church—and it is the head that tells the body what to do. The body finds its definition for who it is by being connected to the head.

...holding fast to the Head, from whom all the body, nourished and knit together by joints and ligaments, grows with the increase which is from God.
                                    Colossians 2:19

Jesus is the Head of the Church; we are the Body of the Church. Jesus does not want a spastic body where arms, legs, and other members go off in different directions without any sense of coordination.

It is the headship of Jesus that gives unity and coordination to the Church. Thus the only way we will have unity in the Church is to restore Jesus to His place of top priority. If Jesus is the top priority in every congregation, then the universal Church will be supernaturally unified and coordinated.

Again, we cannot have unity unless Jesus is the Head of the Church. But we cannot have Jesus as the Head of the Church unless we are willing to submit to being unified. Jesus' role as Head of the Church demands that the rest of us to come into unity. If we do not have a vision for the unity of the Church, then Jesus cannot function fully as the Head of our ministry.

The Body's ligaments and joints are knit together by holding fast to the Head—and the Head directs the ligaments and joints to be knit together. The Headship of Jesus demands the unity of the Church. So if we are to submit to the Lordship of Jesus, then we must submit to His design to bring the Church into unity. To submit to Jesus is to submit to the unity of the Church. In order for Jesus to be the Head of the Church, the Body must come into unity. To worship Jesus as the Head of the Church is also to yield to the unity of the Body.

Becoming Christlike

God's destiny for each one of us as an individual is to become more like Jesus. We become more like Jesus by focusing our attention on Him.

For whom He foreknew, He also predestined to be conformed to the image of His Son, that He might be the firstborn among many brethren.
Romans 8:29

Not only are we to be conformed to the image of Jesus, but we are also as one "among many brethren." In other words, we are destined to become like Jesus not only as individuals, but also as a group. Our Christlikeness is both corporate and individual.

When we ask what God's will is for our life, the answer is straightforward: to be more like Jesus. When we ask what God's will is for the Church, the answer is the same: Christlikeness. The Church as a whole is to manifest more and more of the character of Christ. We, as a body of people, are to be conformed to His image.

Till we all come to the unity of the faith and of the knowledge of the Son of God, to a perfect man, to the measure of the stature of the fullness of Christ.
Ephesians 4:13

Just as an individual becomes more like Christ by focusing on Him, so also does the Church become more like Christ by focusing on Him.

But we all, with unveiled face, beholding as in a mirror the glory of the Lord, are being transformed into the same image from glory to glory....
2 Corinthians 3:18

This verse says we are all to be transformed. The word *all* can be taken two ways. First, it means *each individual*. Each one of us is to be transformed to the image of Christ. But the word *all* also means "together as a group." If we are all to be transformed into the image of Jesus, then we must be doing it together.

If we all head toward the same goal, then we all will end up in the same place. Likewise, it is the *same* image that we are being conformed to. It follows that if we are being conformed to the same image, then we will be the same. Personal consecration to Jesus leads to Christlikeness. If my personal consecration leads me to Christlikeness and your personal consecration leads you to Christlikeness, then ultimately our mutual consecration to God will lead us to become one.

The road of personal consecration to Jesus leads to being unified with other believers. This road to unity is, for each one of us, to be personally consecrated to becoming more like Jesus every day.

Focusing on Jesus

I make it a regular habit in my personal devotions to focus my imagination upon the face of Jesus. I find that this kind of intimacy and imaging has a transforming effect upon my soul and spirit. As I focus on Jesus, my attitudes are purified. Siminarly, as Jesus becomes the focal point of the imaginations of our heart, the character and personality of Jesus grows up within us.

As personal devotional time is to the individual believer, so is the corporate worship experience for the body of the Church. In this worship we are to focus our attention upon Jesus. As we focus our attention upon Him as a group, we become like Him as a group, and are thereby unified.

Worship centered on Jesus causes the Church as a whole to become more Christlike. Jesus-centered worship is also the primary way for us to become unified.

Our intimacy with Jesus brings us into unity. Thus our unity with one another is an inherent part of the experience of intimacy with God.

Run Without Hindrance

There is something about focusing upon Jesus that releases a new freedom and victory in our walk with God.

...let us lay aside every weight, and the sin which so easily ensnares us, and let us run with endurance the race that is set before us, looking unto Jesus, the author and finisher of our faith....
Hebrews 12:1-2

The world, the flesh, and the devil constantly try to get us entangled in their ways in order to bring us down.

If we are to run the race of faith with joy, however, we must be freed from everything that weighs us down. The key to being freed from the snares of this world is to focus our attention upon Jesus. It is the mind whose thoughts are fixed and stayed upon God that will experience peace (see Is. 26:3).

Just as focusing our attention upon Jesus is the key to experiencing spiritual freedom for the individual, so it is true for the Church as a whole. The more we as a corporate body focus our attention upon Jesus, the more the Church will experience freedom and victory. Then as the Church makes Christ preeminent in all things, a new wave of spiritual power is released among us. For the higher the priority that Jesus becomes in the Church, the less the world will be able to pull us down to its level.

We should not let any sin pull us away from Jesus. Neither should we allow any of the concerns of everyday life draw our attention away from Jesus. This includes a particular emphasis of a Church movement or ministry, for even it can divert us from our primary focus on Jesus.

When the Church as a whole puts its full attention upon the person of Jesus, we will experience a new spiritual freedom together, and so will be brought into unity. If the Church is to be all that God wants us to be, we must return to the simplicity of Jesus.

Chapter 6

Jewish Roots

The Body of Christ is described as a vine or a tree. Jesus Himself is the vine, and we are the branches that compose the vine.

I am the true vine, and My Father is the vinedresser. ...
I am the vine, you are the branches....
John 15:1,5

I used to think this passage said that Jesus was the trunk of the tree, and we were the branches. That is to say, He is the starting point and we are the extensions of who He is. The trunk is one thing; the branches are another. But the passage contains an even stronger metaphor. Jesus is the total vine encompassing all the trunk and branches; we are the various segments that make up who He is. He is composed of us, His people.

That is a metaphor; we are not actually Jesus. The point is, the Scriptures use the strongest possible language to indicate our complete union with Him. We are part of who He is.

The Olive Tree

The Body of Christ is described not only as a vine, but also as an olive tree. In this metaphor, the unifying factor of the olive tree/Church is not Jesus, but the nation of Israel. Israel is described as the root; the other sections of the Church, coming from various Gentile nations, are referred to as branches.

> *For if the firstfruit is holy, the lump is also holy; and if the root is holy, so are the branches.*
>
> Romans 11:16

The first people who became believers in Jesus were Jewish. They are described here as "firstfruits." Since the believers who lived before Jesus were also primarily Jewish, the classic history of the nation of Israel is described here as the "root."

The root or firstfruit was holy because there were dedicated believers among the Israelites. It is not that the Jews themselves are holy, but that they had a holy faith in a holy God. The firstfruits made the rest of the plant holy because the faith among the Jews spread to people of other national groups. If there had been no faith among the Jews, there could have been no faith to spread to the

Gentiles. Thus the branches could not have been made holy unless the root was holy.

...Because of unbelief they were broken off, and you stand by faith....
Romans 11:20

It was the faith resident among the Jews that made them part of God's tree; it was their faith that made them holy. Their chosenness is not a matter of racial preference but of a heritage of making covenant with God. God is not a respecter of persons, but He is a respecter of faithfulness to His covenants.

Both Jews and Gentiles become grafted into the olive tree of God according to their faith. Both Jews and Gentiles are removed from the olive tree by their unbelief.

And if some of the branches were broken off, and you, being a wild olive tree, were grafted in among them, and with them became a partaker of the root and fatness of the olive tree.
Romans 11:17

When people from Gentile nations became believers in the God of Abraham, they were grafted into the historic olive tree that, until that time, had been composed primarily of believers from among the Jews. To become a believer was seen as joining into the heritage and history of the people who were already believers.

One People of God

In God's eyes, there always has been one people of God. There has been only one olive tree. When Gentiles became believers, they were grafted into that olive tree; they did not go off and start a different kind of tree somewhere else. Neither were the Gentile believers seen as destroying or replacing the olive tree, but rather being joined together with it.

The Gentile believers became partakers, or participants, of the continuing, historic tree of faith. That olive tree, however, has Jewish roots. It always has and it always will.

The new believers, coming from every nation, were not to feel like "second class" citizens in the Kingdom of God. Each person is an equal member. But neither were they to be haughty or sectarian. There was a sense of equality, but also a sense of gratefulness and appreciation for the people who had held fast to the covenant before them.

Believers from every nation had a sense of identification with the nation of Israel and its biblical heritage. They were "partakers of the olive tree." This sense of identification with Israel was meant to be maintained. Christians everywhere are to have a spiritual identification with the history and people of Israel. Since this identification with Israel is a common element among all believers, it also serves as a unifying element. It is a thread of historic, cultural, and spiritual unity for the Church.

Jewish Roots

The Commonwealth

Therefore remember that you, once Gentiles in the flesh...that at that time you were without Christ, being aliens from the commonwealth of Israel and strangers from the covenants of promise, having no hope and without God in the world. But now in Christ Jesus you who once were far off have been bought near by the blood of Christ.

Ephesians 2:11-13

This passage uses the image of a commonwealth instead of an olive tree to describe the same idea. In a commonwealth, one nation extends its range of citizenship and dominion into other nations. In the British Commonwealth, for example, England extended her governing influence and national identity to many other nations.

Faith in Jesus was seen as bringing the Gentile peoples into a covenant with the God of Israel and with the people of Israel. The Gentiles had been far from the God of Israel and the people of Israel. However, they were brought near to the God of Israel and the people of Israel by the blood of the Messiah. When they came to believe in Israel's God, they felt a sense of affinity and loyalty to the nation as well.

Ruth's Twofold Confession

A twofold covenant takes place through faith in Jesus. The primary part of the covenant is with God Himself;

the secondary part is with the people of God. The covenant demands loyalty to the remnant of believers in every nation and to the extended national heritage from which the faith originated.

> *But Ruth said, "...For wherever you go, I will go; and wherever you lodge, I will lodge; your people shall be my people, and your God, my God."*
> Ruth 1:16

Naomi (a Jewish believer) had two Gentile daughters-in-law who came to believe in the God of Israel. Orpah decided to identify herself only with the people of her own national background. Ruth, however, made this significant twofold confession of loyalty: not only would Israel's God be her God, but Israel's people would be her people. Her motivation for this commitment was not that she felt "Jewish," but that she had a deep sense of kinship for the people who led her to the Lord.

Ruth serves as a symbolic example for Christian identification with the people of Israel. This identification carries a special blessing. Ruth took the courageous step of identification with the nation of Israel and became one of the key figures in the lineage of the Messiah.

Balance of Attitude Toward the Jews

We need a balance in attitude toward the Jewish people. Christians should not despise them, but neither should they idolize them. The Jews should not be rejected in a form of Christian anti-Semitism; nor should they be glorified in a type of reverse racism that says a Jewish person is closer to God simply because he is physically Jewish.

Christians have demonstrated much extremism and confusion in their attitudes toward the Jews. One extreme would be typified by the "Church replacement" doctrine, which says God has done away with His purposes for the nation of Israel and has replaced it with a Gentile institution called the Church. Meanwhile, the Jewish people are relegated to a kind of mongrel race in a cursed condition.

The other extreme is typified by the "Two Covenant" doctrine, which says God has a separate way of dealing with Jewish people through the Mosaic Law and Abrahamic Covenant to such a degree that they do not need to come to faith in Jesus as their Messiah in order to be saved.

Some Christians are defensive against God's calling upon the nation of Israel. They overreact and reject God's role for the Jews by interpreting Scriptures in such a way as to ignore the many passages describing the importance of the restoration and revival of Israel. Other Christians overreact in the opposite direction. They become so enamored of Jewish people that they wish they were Jews. Some even go to the extreme of fabricating evidence of Jewish lineage in their family background and pretending they are Jewish.

Positive and Negative

Both of these types of reactions are incorrect. There is a balance to the scriptural evaluation of the role of the Jewish people.

Concerning the gospel they are enemies for your sake, but concerning the election they are beloved for the sake of the fathers. For the gifts and the calling of God are irrevocable.

Romans 11:28-29

Both a positive and a negative element exists in the history of the Jews. The negative element is they have consistently set themselves in opposition to the preaching of the gospel. That opposition comes from orthodox Jewish religious objections to Christian claims that Jesus is the Messiah as well as from liberal Jewish humanists' demands for the separation of any kind of religion from a secular society. The positive element is the many-faceted history of the Jewish people as stewards of the covenants and oracles of God (see Rom. 9:4-5). God has a calling upon the Jewish people to be a priestly race among the nations. We Jews have largely disobeyed that calling, but the calling of God remains the same. In the long run God will see to it that this calling for the Jews is fulfilled.

David and Joseph

God's role for the Jewish people will only make sense to Christians when significant numbers of Jewish people return to faith in Jesus as their Messiah. From God's point of view, it is a gross abnormality for the Jews not to believe in Jesus. After all, Jesus is the King of the Jews. For the Jews to reject Him is tantamount to a divorce within the national family. The nation derives its meaning and purpose from the Messiahship of Jesus.

The Jewish nation will not come into its glorious destiny until it receives Jesus as Messiah. Consider this historical example. David had already been anointed by God as king, but most of the nation rejected him and adhered to the leadership of Saul. As long as Saul was the leader instead of David, the nation lived in a disrupted condition. In the course of time, however, they did receive David as their king. With David as the leader, Israel soon developed into a prosperous commonwealth.

So it will be with the Jews in relation to Jesus. Jesus has already been appointed as their King. However, they have rejected Him. Because of that rejection, they have lived in a condition of disgrace. Even as Judah was the last tribe to receive David when the other tribes had already recognized him as king, so the Jews will be the last people in this gospel age to recognize Jesus as Messiah. But recognize Him they will. When they do, Israel and the Church will merge together into one glorious commonwealth that will manifest the Kingdom of God on the earth.

A similar situation is seen in the life of Joseph. He was anointed by God to be the leader of the children of Israel and of the Egyptian empire. Nevertheless, his own brothers rejected him out of jealousy. Thus Joseph went down into a pit and then was raised to become governor of Egypt. Everyone in the world recognized that he was the leader except for his Israelite brethren. During the time

The Five Streams

they rejected Joseph, his brothers lived in shame and turmoil. Finally Joseph was revealed to his own kinsmen, and they entered into a new state of blessing and harmony.

So it will happen at the end of this age. Jesus will be revealed to the Jews as their Messiah—and that revelation will bring blessing and harmony to the whole world.

The Messianic Movement

The gifts and callings of the Jews come into a positive expression when they believe in Jesus. The Jews' return to faith in Jesus is clearly prophesied throughout Scriptures. Even the timing is indicated. Paul said that the Jews would begin to believe in Jesus when the age of the Gentiles was fulfilled (see Rom. 11:25). Jesus said that the age of the Gentiles would come to an end when, after a long period of desolation, Jerusalem would finally come back into the hands of the Jews (see Lk. 21:24).

Jerusalem was recaptured in 1967. Previous to 1967 there were very few Jewish believers in Jesus. Since 1967, however, there has sprouted a widespread grassroots movement of Messianic Jews. Today there are more than a hundred Messianic fellowships in the United States. No individual or organization can claim credit for engineering this movement. Its variegated and explosive appearance can only be explained by the fact that it is a sovereign move of God.

The Scriptures exhibit a pattern concerning the role that the Church and Israel have together in manifesting the Kingdom of God upon the earth. I would summarize that pattern in these four words: restoration, remnant, revival, and return. These words refer to the restoration of the international Body of Christ (primarily Gentile), which brings about the salvation of a remnant of Jewish believers in Jesus, which in turn is the catalyst for an end-times revival in the land of Israel, which is the last event to take place and leads to the return of Jesus and the resurrection of the dead.

Restoration of the Church

First, the Church must be restored to the purposes and functions that God designed for it. The gospel must be preached to all the nations of the world (see Mt. 24:14). God's plans for Israel and the Second Coming start with the Church coming into its full destiny of purity and glory. This is what Paul meant by "magnifying" his ministry to the Gentiles.

> *For I speak to you Gentiles; inasmuch as I am an apostle to the Gentiles, I magnify my ministry.*
> Romans 11:13

As a Jewish believer, and as one who has a particular calling to work for revival in Israel, I am aware that any ministry to the Jews is predicated on the fullness of the Gentile Church. One of Paul's motivations for ministering to the Gentiles was his desire to see the Kingdom of God restored to Israel (see Acts 1:6). If there is to be a spiritual restoration to the nation of Israel, it will be due

The Five Streams

to the dynamic life of the Kingdom of God manifested through the Gentile Church.

Remnant of Messianic Jews

As the Church comes to its fullness, a number of Jews will be attracted to the gospel.

If by any means I may provoke to jealousy those who are my flesh and save some of them.

Romans 11:14

This will not be a large number at the beginning. Paul describes an interaction whereby "some" of the Jews are attracted to the faith by the Church. That initial remnant of Jews who come to faith in Jesus is already appearing around the world. This movement, called Messianic Judaism, Jews for Jesus, or Hebrew Christianity, is a fulfillment of this verse in answer to Paul's prayer that some Jews would get saved.

Revival in Israel

This present remnant of Jewish believers in Jesus will continue to grow until it blossoms into a full-fledged revival in the land of Israel.

And so all Israel will be saved....

Romans 11:26

It may seem difficult to imagine such a sweep of evangelism in the modern nation of Israel. The Jewish social and religious structure has historically been opposed to faith in Jesus. However, we have a clear biblical promise that such a revival will take place.

This coming revival in Israel is what Paul refers to as "all Israel" being saved. It does not mean every Jew will be saved simply because he is Jewish; nor does it mean every Jew alive today will be saved. It does mean that after the wars and tribulations of the endtimes (which include large numbers of Jews being killed [see Zech. 13:8]), a national repentance will sweep across Israel, in which virtually the entire nation will turn to faith in Jesus.

If there is to be such a revival in Israel, it is obvious that God must bring the people back to the land in the first place. Thus the prophecies of the restoration of Israel have two stages. First the Jews are regathered physically; then they are revived spiritually (see Ezek. 37). The fact that so many Jews have returned to the land of Israel today is a miraculous fulfillment of prophecy. If the first stage of prophecy is being fulfilled, the second stage cannot be far behind. If the Jews are being regathered physically to the land, then the spiritual revival is soon to follow.

Return of Jesus

This revival in Israel, which takes place concurrent with the battle of Armageddon, is the culmination of the battle of good and evil upon the earth. It represents the final and greatest victory of the mission of the Gentile Church. The widespread salvation of the Jews will be the event that ushers in the Second Coming of Jesus the Messiah.

> *For if their being cast away is the reconciling of the world, what will their acceptance be but life from the dead?*
>
> Romans 11:15

With this sweeping revival in Israel, Jesus will return and the dead shall be raised. The government of the Messiah's Kingdom will be established on the earth. In short, the restoration and full glory of the Church ultimately leads to the Second Coming of Christ. When the fullness of the Church leads to Israel's salvation, it is Israel's salvation that leads to the millennial kingdom.

Humility for Jews and Gentiles

God is arranging history in such a way that the Gentiles need the Jews and the Jews need the Gentiles. Neither one can do without the other. Humility on the part of the Jews toward the Gentiles is necessary if they are to receive Jesus as their Messiah. Humility on the part of the Gentiles toward the Jews is necessary for the Second Coming of Christ and the resurrection of the dead.

> *For I do not desire, brethren, that you should be ignorant of this mystery, lest you should be wise in your own opinion, that blindness in part has happened to Israel until the fullness of the Gentiles has come in.*
>
> Romans 11:25

Jewish Roots

The key to Israel's being saved (verse 26) is the Gentiles' not being "wise in their own conceits" (verse 25). As Gentile Christians repent of their pride and their rejection of God's calling upon the Jews, the blindness that has kept the Jews from believing in Jesus will be lifted from their eyes. The Jews then will have to repent of their pride to admit that Christians have been correct in claiming that Jesus is the Messiah.

It is amazing how God will work all these elements together in such a way that He Himself will receive the glory (see Rom. 11:33).

Diversity of Cultural Expression

The Body of Christ should allow for the expression of cultural and racial heritages of people from every background. The fact that the Church is to be unified does not mean that we all are to be uniform. God's unity comes through diversity. If we are to have harmony and unity among people who are different, we must make room for these differences to be expressed.

One of the beautiful characteristics of the Church is its demonstration of racial reconciliation. In the Church can be seen a manifestation of the differing gifts and callings that exist in every ethnic group.

> *There is neither Jew nor Greek, there is neither slave nor free, there is neither male nor female; for you are all one in Christ Jesus.*
>
> Galatians 3:28

We all become one in the Messiah. However, that oneness does not mean women are to act like men and men like women. Our unity does not come from suppressing someone else's differences, but from allowing others full freedom of expression to be who God called them to be. It is in the Body of Christ that men can be men and women can be women. We have unity because we encourage one another to express our different identities.

The Rainbow

Blacks can be Blacks; Whites can be Whites; Jews can be Jews; Orientals can be Orientals; and so on. It is a beautiful thing to see all these differences expressed harmoniously. We could say that God is the conductor of our orchestra of faith. The beauty of the symphony is the way in which the sounds are blended together. There would be unity if every instrument in the orchestra were the same, but there would be no beauty. The beauty is found in the harmony. Harmony demands that there be different elements and that those elements cooperate with one another.

The first symbol God chose to express His covenant with the nations was a rainbow. The rainbow is the symbol of the international Church; it is an excellent portrayal of beauty through harmony and unity through diversity. If the rainbow was composed of only one color, it would not have the striking beauty that it does. If the colors of the rainbow were scattered in every direction in conflict and confusion, there would be no beauty.

The beauty of the rainbow comes from the different colors that are unified. The colors must be different—and the colors must come together. So it is with the Church. The colors represent the cultural expressions of the different racial and ethnic groups. In order for the Body of Christ to reveal its beauty, different cultural expressions should be encouraged.

God made the different nations and ethnic groups; He is the Father of the nations (see Acts 17:26). He made each people group with different qualitites. Since He made us different, it must have been His intention for us to express those differences within His Kingdom.

Guidelines for Diversity

Here are three guidelines for expressing the variety of culture and heritage harmoniously.

1. Multiracial—Every congregation should be multiracial to some degree. Racial reconciliation demonstrates the power of the Kingdom of God that causes people to love one another. No congregation will have all racial groups represented, but every congregation should have at least one area of racial reconciliation incorporated into its church body.

2. Primary culture—Although each congregation is multiracial, one primary culture will emerge, which is the calling of that local assembly to express. That primary cultural expression will likely match the largest population group within the congregation. Each local congregation then is a gift to the greater Body of Christ as an example of their particular calling and culture.

3. Israelite identity—As each congregation will have a different expression of racial reconciliation and primary culture, one common thread for all will be an element of Jewish identity. Although other racial and cultural expressions are due to the mixture of population surrounding the local assembly, the element of Jewish identity is related to the history of God's covenant, which is common to every believer.

For example, an Hispanic church will express its primary culture as Spanish. If the church is located in suburban America, it is likely to have a demonstration of reconciliation between Whites and Hispanics. A predominantly White church might primarily express its American heritage, but it should also incorporate a ministry of Black and White reconciliation. A Messianic congregation, whose primary cultural calling is Jewish, will demonstrate reconciliation between Jew and Gentile.

Every congregation, whether White, Black, Hispanic, or Oriental, even if it does not have one Jewish member, can still express an element of identification with Israel. As believers in Jesus, all members have the common heritage of the Law, the Prophets, and the early Church. Since Bible prophecies deal with the restoration of modern Israel as well, churches everywhere can express, as part of their general Christian culture, a degree of identification and loyalty with modern Israel.

The Unifying Branch

We have said that, in the Scriptures, the Church is described as a vine or tree. Jesus is the vine—He is the primary unifying element of the branches, who are individual believers throughout the world (see Jn. 15). The Church is also described as an olive tree. The root or stalk is the nation of Israel, while the various branches are the different Gentile nations. The root of Israel (that is, the common heritage of all Christians found in the history of Israel) provides a base of unity in which the other branches can come together.

Do not boast against the branches. But if you do boast, remember that you do not support the root, but the root supports you.
                                    Romans 11:18

All the branches of a tree are connected to the trunk. No one branch can claim to be a common linkage for the other branches; only the trunk can become a rallying point for unity among the other branches. Thus neither the Hispanic, Caucasian, African, or Oriental branches of the Church represent a common heritage with the other branches. There is no vehicle for mutual identification. However, the Jewish root of the Church (because the early members of the Church were Jewish) provides a potential rallying point for cultural and spiritual identification for the Body of Christ.

The Faith of Abraham

All of us as believers in Jesus, regardless of our background, walk in the footsteps of the faith of our father Abraham.

...that the promise might be sure to all the seed, not only to those who are of the law, but also to those who are of the faith of Abraham, who is the father of us all.
Romans 4:16

Muslims, Christians, and Jews all look to Abraham as their father. Old Abraham has quite a family on his hands!

It is not so much the man himself as it is the faith of Abraham that we follow (see Rom. 11:20). Having the same kind of faith that Abraham had grafts us into unity with God and with other believers. However, faith cannot be divorced from the historical figures who walked in faith. If we follow the faith of Abraham, there is also a certain loyalty to Abraham himself and to his descendants. Faith and faithfulness go together.

The universal Body of Christ derives its primary unity from its spiritual connection with Jesus. Since the various sections of the Church all stem from a common Jewish root, the heritage of Israel provides a secondary basis of identification and unity for Christians everywhere.

Chapter 7

Oneness With God

The Church also is described as the Bride of Christ. We are to become one with God spiritually even as Adam and Eve became one with each other physically.

Or do you not know that he who is joined to a harlot is one body with her? For "the two," He says, "shall become one flesh." But he who is joined to the Lord is one spirit with Him.

1 Corinthians 6:16-17

Our human spirit is designed to become one with God's Spirit. Each believer becomes one with God in spirit. The Church, the people of God as a whole, is also designed to become one in spirit with God.

The Bride of Christ

Through faith in Jesus, we are married to God. Faith is a covenant just as marriage is a covenant. God has married us, our relationship to God is similar to that of a wife to her husband. This is a great mystery, Paul said.

"For this reason a man shall leave his father and mother and be joined to his wife, and the two shall become one flesh." This is a great mystery, but I speak concerning Christ and the church.
Ephesians 5:31-32

The mystery is that God purposely designed the relationship between husband and wife to be a model of the relationship He desires with us. Considering the depth of feelings that men have for women, it is startling to think that it is a portrait of how God feels about us.

Once while in prayer I asked the Lord about the problems that lust causes in human society. I could not understand how God would create a desire so strong that many people would lose control because of it. (Lust, of course, is a perverse overreaction to the wholesome attraction between men and women that God designed.) The Lord reminded me of these passages. The desire a man has for a woman is so strong because it indicates how strong God's desire is to become one with His people.

God is a jealous God. He is jealous as a husband is jealous over his wife. He fiercely guards the relationship of intimacy. Thus sin can be defined as any action or attitude that violates intimacy with God. God's wrath is poured out upon sin as a jealous husband would become

Oneness With God

furious at a wife's betrayal. (This explains why the curse against unfaithfulness in marriage [see Num. 5] is directed only against the woman. The passage is rightly understood in light of the symbolism of God and His people.)

Like Adam and Eve

When God created Adam, He said it was not good for Adam to be alone (see Gen. 2:18). God created a mate or companion for Adam. The relationship between Adam and Eve was similar to what God wanted with the human race. In a figurative sense, it is not good for God to be alone. It is right for Him to have a companion. As God created Eve to be a marriage partner for Adam, so He created us to be His marriage partner.

The animals, trees, and rocks were not sufficient companions for Adam. Adam needed someone more like himself with whom to share fellowship. Eve was created different from Adam, yet she was like him in many ways. Similarly, God created mankind in His likeness. God made Eve from Adam; we were created in God's image. When Adam first saw Eve, he was excited at the prospect of sharing fellowship with her.

And Adam said: "This is now bone of my bones and flesh of my flesh...."
Genesis 2:23

The Church is married to God. The people of God are to serve as a wifely companion to God. The passages in the Bible that speak of the enjoyable relationship between husband and wife can be taken as symbolizing the relationship God wants to have with us.

The lover and the beloved in the Song of Solomon are figures of Messiah and His people. Isaac playing with Rebecca, Ezekiel's calling his wife the desire of his eyes (see Ezek. 24:16), and the romance between David and Abigail are a few examples of biblical images of marriages that reflect back upon our relationship with God.

Intimacy and Purity

As a bride is sometimes pictured as staring at her husband in adoration and respect, so is the Church to focus its attention upon Jesus. Jesus is the Head of the Church as a man is the head of his wife.

> *For the husband is head of the wife, as also Christ is head of the Church....*
>
> Ephesians 5:23

Jesus' headship demands that the Church become more pure and holy. Jesus' headship also demands that we share intimacy with Him.

> *That He might sanctify and cleanse her* [the Church] *with the washing of water by the word, that He might present her to Himself a glorious church, not having spot or wrinkle or any such thing, but that she should be holy and without blemish.*
>
> Ephesians 5:26-27

Oneness With God

Jesus is preparing a Bride for Himself. His Bride is to be neither a harlot nor a harem girl. He is purging us of both sin and strife; He is calling us to purity and unity. He redeems us as a woman who fell into adultery and immorality. He trains us and cleanses us to restore a state of virgin-like purity and faithfulness to Him.

None of us were spiritual virgins. We all fell into sin. In His unfailing faithfulness and mercy, God decided not to reject us. He sent Jesus to the earth to die for us and to cleanse us of our sins. He continues to work with us until we are finally made pure and whole in His sight.

God told Hosea to marry a prostitute in order to demonstrate how He draws us back to Himself (see Hos. 1-2). Hosea needed many days to train his wife out of her whorish habits of unfaithfulness. So it is that God patiently and firmly continues the discipleship process of training us out of our unfaithful habits. If we turn back to unfaithfulness, however, God's wrath is poured out on us as upon an adulterous lover who has betrayed her mate (see Ezek. 16).

The Body of Christ

The Church is described not only as the Bride of Christ, but also as His Body. Consider how man is a spirit being that inhabits a physical body. The spirit and soul of man fit inside his body like a hand inside a glove. So it is that the Spirit of God dwells within us.

For we are members of His body, of His flesh and of His bones.
                                                        Ephesians 5:30

We are pictured as the members and organs of Jesus' body. Jesus Himself is in Heaven; He has His own resurrected body. He is not a disembodied spirit. However, when we receive Jesus as Lord, His Spirit enters us in a way similar to which His Spirit dwells in His own body.

Thus if we all have the Spirit of God through Jesus, then we all have the same Spirit. If Jesus dwells in us, we must be one because we have the same Spirit.

> *Do you not know that you are the temple of God and that the Spirit of God dwells in you?*
> 1 Corinthians 3:16

We are the dwelling place of God. We are His temple, His physical habitation upon this planet. God extends His spiritual presence throughout the earth by dwelling in us. Thus the Spirit of God inhabits His people; God's innermost being dwells within us. To say that we are the Body of Christ, then, means we are the extensions of the very life and personality of Jesus.

> *I am the vine, you are the branches....*
> John 15:5

We are part of who He is; we extend His presence. His mind is in our mind (see 1 Cor. 2:16). He sees through our eyes; He walks around with us.

The Church Is to Be Like Jesus

We are to become more like Jesus every day. Not only are we to become more like Him as individuals, but we

Oneness With God

together as the Church are to become more like Him as well.

Beloved, now we are children of God; and it has not yet been revealed what we shall be, but we know that when He is revealed, we shall be like Him, for we shall see Him as He is.

1 John 3:2

...as He is, so are we in this world.

1 John 4:17

It is not just that I will be like Jesus and you will be like Jesus. *We together* will be like Jesus. So are "we" in this world. Individual believers do manifest the image of Jesus. But the Church is to manifest the image of Jesus as well.

It has not yet been revealed all that we shall be as the Church. We do know that the Church will be like Him. As Jesus is, so is the Church in this world. The Body of Christ manifests the presence of Jesus in the world. As the Body of Christ we carry the corporate anointing and spirit of the Kingdom of God. We have in us now the deposit of the power of the age to come (see Heb. 6:5; 2 Cor. 1:22).

Jesus, the Only Foundation

Jesus is in the process of joining us together. He is doing this so the Spirit of God can reside in us as a corporate body. The Spirit of God dwells in each one of us individually, and He can manifest Himself through any one of us. But the potential manifestation of the corporate anointing of God is greater than the sum of the parts. (A fist is greater than the sum of five fingers.) As we come into spiritual unity, the Spirit of God can manifest Himself in a way greater than has ever before been seen.

> *...Jesus Christ Himself being the chief cornerstone, in whom the whole building...grows into a holy temple in the Lord, in whom you also are being built together for a dwelling place of God in the Spirit.*
> Ephesians 2:20-22

If we are to have unity, we must recognize that Jesus is the cornerstone of the Church. He is the only foundation upon which the Church can be built.

> *For no other foundation can anyone lay than that which is laid, which is Jesus Christ.*
> 1 Corinthians 3:11

Most of us acknowledge the doctrine that Jesus is the foundation of the Church. The question is whether or not He is the ongoing priority in each aspect of the ministry. Have our programs gotten ahead of the centrality of Jesus? Are we building our ministries on some doctrine or movement other than on Jesus? Any project that does not put Jesus first will ultimately fail, and will not work toward the unity of the Church.

Union With God Before Unity With People

Jesus abides in us, and we abide in Him. He is the vine and we are the branches of that vine. His life is the sap that runs through the branches. Our unity is borne out

Oneness With God

of the fact that we dwell in Him and He dwells in us. Thus we only have unity with one another if we first experience oneness with God.

> *...that you also may have fellowship with us; and truly our fellowship is with the Father and with His Son Jesus Christ.*
> 1 John 1:3

First we establish intimacy with God. Out of that intimate fellowship, others are invited to join us. So the source of our unity is our oneness with Him. We have fellowship with one another as we experience spiritual communion with God. Our first mode of fellowship is not eating and socializing, but prayer and worship.

> *But if we walk in the light as He is in the light, we have fellowship with one another....*
> 1 John 1:7

People who have prayed and worshiped together experience a level of fellowship that others cannot know. Those who have been together in the anointing and presence of God have shared an intimacy that can come from no other experience. If we seek to have deeper communion with one another, let us do so by pressing forward together into a deeper spiritual walk with God.

Oneness With God

It is our spiritual oneness with God that produces unity among us as brethren.

That they all may be one, as You, Father, are in Me, and I in You; that they also may be one in Us.... And the glory which You gave Me I have given them, that they may be one just as We are one: I in them, and You in Me; that they may be made perfect in one....
John 17:21-23

We have discussed these verses in the light of our unity with one another. However, these verses do not primarily talk about our horizontal unity within the Church, but about the vertical experience of our oneness with God. These verses describe the opportunity that each one of us has to become one spirit with God. Unity with one another is a byproduct of that oneness with God.

Jesus is praying for you and me that we can become one with God the Father as He is. Jesus is inviting us to have Him dwell in us the same way the Father dwells in Him. We can dwell in God, and God can dwell in us. Faith in Jesus allows us to become one with God even as Jesus and God are one with each other. Jesus' prayer is for us to experience the awesome miracle of oneness with God.

He in Us, We in Him

Jesus dwells in us. Thus, if we are spiritually sensitive, we can often perceive His desires and inclinations within our hearts. We can perceive that subtle grace by which we know He is pleased with one thing and displeased with another. We can know what He is thinking and feeling at any given moment. We are in contact with Him as He dwells inside of us.

Oneness With God

As a rough example, this indwelling might be likened to the way a picture appears on a television set. The person may be in a studio miles away, but we see the figure, the color, and the motion in our own living room. Similarly, Jesus Himself is in Heaven, but we can perceive His character and personality stirring within us. Somehow we know that He is in there.

On the other hand, we are in Him too. He is praying for us in Heaven. Just as we can perceive His spiritual presence, so He can perceive ours. He is easily touched with our infirmities (see Heb. 4:15). He is grieved when we sin. He experiences joy when we walk in the Spirit. He perceives our actions within His innermost being. As we pick up His wavelength, so to speak, on the receiver of our heart, so He picks up ours.

Just as He is in us, so are we in Him. As a mother prays for her children, her children dwell spiritually within her heart. Mothers who intercede for their children are often intuitively aware when their children are in some kind of danger.

So it is with a pastor who prays for his congregation. He is grieved for their sins and he rejoices when they walk in love.

For though I am absent in the flesh, yet I am with you in spirit, rejoicing to see your good order and the steadfastness of your faith in Christ.

Colossians 2:5

Who is weak, and I am not weak? Who is made to stumble, and I do not burn with indignation?

2 Corinthians 11:29

As a mother's children abide spiritually in her heart and as a pastor's congregants abide in his heart, so do we all spiritually abide in the heart of Jesus.

Oneness With God Causes Unity

What does all this have to do with the unity of the Church? Let us suppose that I am a person who cares very little about having fellowship with you. All I care about is my fellowship with Jesus. My only goal in life is to experience oneness with God. I want Jesus to dwell in my heart in all of His fullness. I might even say, "Jesus, I do not care about other people. What I want is for You to come and dwell within me."

The problem is, when I invite Jesus into my heart, you and all the rest of the saints are already in Jesus' heart. I may want Jesus alone, but you come with the package. I want Jesus in my heart, and He already has you in His heart. So if I want Jesus, I am going to have to take you as well. If I want Jesus to dwell in my heart in all of His fullness, I have to realize that He carries you inside Him. I cannot have Jesus without taking you.

Breastplate of Intercession

The High Priest in the ancient tabernacle wore a breastplate inscribed with the names of the tribes of the children of Israel. He went into the Holy of Holies wearing that breastplate. This is a symbolic example of how Jesus carries the burdens of His people into the presence of God through intercession. You cannot separate Jesus the High Priest from His breastplate. The saints of God are always upon His heart.

Oneness With God

It is also worth noting that Jesus cannot be separated from His burden for the tribes of Israel. If the symbolism of the breastplate can be applied to the saints of any nation, it also can be applied to Jesus' continuing intercessory prayer for the Jewish people. Intercession is a priestly function. As we intercede, we bear upon our hearts the love and burden for those for whom we pray. One operates in the priesthood of intercession not only by praying for believers everywhere, but also by having a particular burden for the 12 tribes of Israel, to bring them as an ephod into the presence of God.

Abiding in Each Other

If Jesus dwells in me and if He bears an intercessory awareness of what is happening in your life, then it immediately becomes possible for me to be connected to you in the spirit. Through Jesus, when I pray, I can become aware of the struggles in your life. (This is why the charismatic gifts are connected to prayer and love.) As Jesus abides in me, so will you abide in me. As Jesus abides in you, and as I abide in Jesus, so I will abide in you as well.

This is the secret of how Jesus' prayer in John 17 produces unity among the believers. Our oneness with God cannot help but cause a unity within the Church. As we each abide in Him and He abides in us, we will be abiding in one another. Thus our unity is more than an ecumenical or fraternal cooperation. It is a supernatural miracle of God. Our unity exists in a spiritual dimension beyond the human mind and emotions.

The Five Streams

This is our motivation. We are not people who primarily seek fellowship with other human beings. We are lovers of God. We are bent upon seeking and striving after greater dimensions of union with God. We are partakers of the divine nature (see 2 Pet. 1:4). We hunger and thirst for deeper levels of the infilling of God's Spirit. It is as we press on toward the goal of Christlikeness and oneness with God that we are confronted with the necessity and the challenge of dealing with our unity with one another.

Whether that challenge is a blessing or a curse, whether an opportunity or obstacle, it does not alter the fact that unity stands squarely in the middle of the road leading to communion with God. You have me and I have you. Our love for Jesus compels us into the place where we love one another. It is the love of God that compels us (see 2 Cor. 5:14). If we love God, we must love one another (see 1 Jn. 4:20).

Our Inheritance in the Saints

Our destinies are caught up with one another. My destiny is in Jesus; your destiny is in Jesus. Since Jesus cannot be divided (see 1 Cor. 1:13), neither can our destinies be separated one from another.

God has something special and glorious planned for us. God gives us this glorious inheritance together with the rest of the believers.

> *...that you may know what is the hope of His calling, what are the riches of the glory of His inheritance in the saints.*
>
> Ephesians 1:18

Giving thanks to the Father who has qualified us to be partakers of the inheritance of the saints in the light.
Colossians 1:12

Our inheritance is *in the saints* and of *the saints*. If we are to receive our inheritance, then we must receive it together. God has given His glory to us as the children of His family—and we do not want to be children who fight and bicker over the family's inheritance. God bestows His blessing upon us as a group, as well as individuals.

If we are to enter into our inheritance as children of God, then we must enter into the harmony of the family of believers.

The Mount of Transfiguration

The Kingdom of God will manifest the best elements of all the streams of the Church. How? Jesus once told His disciples that they would see an example of the glory and power of His Kingdom. Then He took some of them to a mountain to pray. As they prayed, Jesus was transfigured before their eyes.

His clothes became shining, exceedingly white, like snow, such as no launderer on earth can whiten them. And Elijah appeared to them with Moses, and they were talking with Jesus.
Mark 9:3-4

All the movements of the Church are represented in this demonstration of the Kingdom. There is purity and power. The saints are drawn into the cloud of glory with Jesus. They are told to focus their attention on Him instead of building their own self-centered structures (see Mk. 9:5-7).

Moses and Elijah represent the Hebrew tradition of the Law and the Prophets. In this manifestation of the Kingdom, they are seen as harmonized with the role of the Messiah. Jesus is seen in proper context as the continuation and fulfillment of the Law and the Prophets.

The Holiness, Messianic, Covenant, Kingdom, and Faith streams of the Church will flow together into a glorious expression of Heaven itself. Then, we are transfigured with Jesus as children of light.

Conclusion

It is our desire for oneness with God that compels us to seek unity with one another. It is through oneness with God that unity with one another will be accomplished.

Thus if we are to become all that God wants us to be, we must be willing to learn what God has to say through one another. The Church will come to unity as we combine the streams of revelation found in the different movements of the Church. As we place our primary emphasis upon Jesus and not upon the agenda of any particular movement in the Church, we will find it easier to be united with one another. Then we will be able to express all the glory and power that God wants for us as the Body of Christ.

Appendix

Other Streams?

Daniel Juster

Any broad evaluation of any aspect of history is necessarily an oversimplification. In speaking of the five streams, Keith Intrater has described broad tendencies or points of identification in the charismatic world. The reader may ask: "Can all movements really be described as part of one of the five streams?" The answer is no. However, those among new movements that are not capable of being so described may actually have elements of many of the other streams. Here are a few categories that can be dealt with in the light of the five streams.

1. Classical Evangelicalism—Evangelicalism is not presently charismatic, although this is changing. Evangelical roots were greatly influenced by the Holiness movements in the nineteenth century. However, evangelical scholarship has sometimes shied away from its

The Five Streams

holiness roots. The anti-intellectual elements of earlier evangelicalism have been repudiated. Yet in the intellectual preoccupations, some evangelicals have lost some of the strengths of their earlier holiness emphases. Today people speak of "worldly evangelicals"! Evangelical Presbyterians never bought the anti-intellectual elements of other evangelicals. The Evangelical movement joins together those from many denominational and independent flows—all of which could be said to be streams of their own, historically.

2. Classical Pentecostalism—Holiness roots not only were foundational to twentieth century evangelicals, but also to the classical pentecostal denominations. These denominations made speaking in tongues *the* sign of the baptism of the Holy Spirit. Classical Pentecostalism has sometimes reacted against the looseness of the Charismatic movement, while others have sought to come into agreement with the charismatics.

3. Latter Rain Movement—From the late 1940's and 1950's this movement emphasized the use of prophetic gifts and the restoration of prophets and apostles. Many classical pentecostals had problems with these emphases. Latter rain emphases today are found in many streams—Kingdom, Covenant, Faith, and Holiness Charismatics! However, there is no identifiable latter rain stream today. Some point to the aberrant "manifest sons" movement as latter rain, but this is really unfair to the "latter rain" since it was a minority offshoot.

4. "Third Wave"—Including the Vineyard movement, this is a movement of many evangelicals who have embraced the gifts of the Spirit. Some charismatics have also connected to the third wave. Third wavers do not identify speaking in tongues as the sign of the Spirit, but accept tongues as a significant gift. However, through Paul Cain and Leonard Ravenhill, there has been a holiness emphasis in the third wave. Without direct influence, third wavers also have emphases that are like Kingdom and Covenant streams. Through Paul Cain's involvement in the healing revival of the 1950's, some would say there are latter rain emphases in the Vineyard and third wave. Vineyard does believe in the restoration of apostles and prophets. However, styles of ministry in the third wave were parallel to some of the styles in the latter rain before their connection to Paul Cain. The third wave tends to reject the Faith stream as unbalanced. It also thinks of itself as seeking to be open to the fullness of spiritual gifts within a context of sounder biblical theology. Yet all streams claim to have the more sound biblical theology!